ONE MAN'S JOURNEY

THE LIFE, LESSONS & LEGACY
OF A WORLD WAR II FIGHTER PILOT

HOWARD "MIKE" SPENCER

WITH KENNETH R. OVERMAN

Edited by Carlyle Carter

Book Cover and Content Design by Patricia Spencer & Katrina Gem Paray

MEDALS AWARDED TO HOWARD (MIKE) SPENCER
FOR HIS WARTIME SERVICE

Air Medal

Distinguished
Flying Cross

French
Legion of Honour

For my grandfather, Alton Mead—my first mentor

CONTENTS

PROLOGUE   13

PART I   THE BEGINNING

Chapter 1   21
Chapter 2   A Solid Foundation   24
              Party Line   27
Chapter 3   Dreaming   30
Chapter 4   My Mentor   32
Chapter 5   Modern Tom Sawyers   35
              Clay Cooking   39
              Maple Syrup   42
Chapter 6   Stretching Up and Out   45

PART II   THE TRAINING YEARS
              JANUARY, 1942 – JUNE, 1944

Chapter 1   Everything Changed   53
              Flight School   56
Chapter 2   My First Solo   59
              Soaring   62
Chapter 3   Graduation   64
              The Dance   67
Chapter 4   Casey   73
Chapter 5   Troop Carrier   77
              Omaha Beach   79
Chapter 6   Thumbing to Paris   81
              The Red Windmill   83

PART III   **ABOVE THE THIRD REICH**

                 JULY, 1944 – OCTOBER 15, 1945

Chapter 1	Plenty of Hours	87
	The Jug	88
	Finally Down to Business	92
Chapter 2	The Shack	95
	A Blind Wingman	99
Chapter 3	Nearly Impenetrable	104
	Sweet Tooth	109
	Warming up the Nurses	112
Chapter 4	He Shook His Fist	115
Chapter 5	Next Stop, Belgium	121
	Getting to Know Her and Myself	122
	Sneaky, Smart, and Damn Competent	123
	In-Flight Conveniences	127
Chapter 6	About Flak	129
	The Bulge	131
	Bastogne	134
	Crimson Pulse	136
Chapter 7	The Death of Marty Lewis	139
	The Flight Surgeon	145
	The Bridge at Remagen	147
	Remorse	149
Chapter 8	What the Hell, Bill!	152
	The Phones Went Dead	155
	I Lost My Tail	156
	Just Take the Autobahn	158
	A Sorrowful Mission	159
Chapter 9	I'll Go Where They Want Me	163
	Marseille	166

PART IV   **A NEW FLIGHT PLAN**
              DECEMBER, 1945 - 2008

Chapter 1	Mr. Spencer	173
	Back to School	176
	The Shadow of Conflict	177
Chapter 2	My First Real Job	179
	Just When Things Were Going So Well	180
	Wine Before Each Mission	182
	Back to the Thread Company	185
	Keeping the Spencers Safe	186
Chapter 3	Marbon Chemicals, Australia	189
	The Unions	190
Chapter 4	It Began in the Cockpit	196
	The Netherlands	198
	Back in Australia	200
	Hong Kong	201
	Transitions	209

PART V   **PLANS FOR MY FUTURE**
              (OR HOW TO LIVE A SATISFYING OLD AGE)

Chapter 1	Basic Ingredients	215
	It's Mostly How You Think	217
	It's Not Just the Wrapper	218
Chapter 2	On Survival	221
	A Word about Goals	221
	It Really is What You Eat	223
Chapter 3	When the Physical Self Won't Cooperate	224
	After Calamity, Move On!	225

EUROPE, 1945
THE SECOND WORLD WAR

⟮ PROLOGUE ⟯

FEBRUARY 14, 1945

15,000 feet above Seigburg, Germany

It looked like an easy target—a German supply train huffing its way across an open valley with a few dozen box and flat cars in tow. It had just emerged from a tunnel into broad daylight, which was strange since the Germans knew we were looking for them. It could be troops, food supplies, or armaments. It didn't matter, since it was our job to take out the train regardless. My only concern was Allied POWs. Were any on board? There was no way to tell. I could only hope our intel was correct. From fifteen thousand feet in clear weather, it would be a good run, so as squadron leader I decided to go in for the attack.

I radioed Lieutenant Kuhl and Captain Lewis in the accompanying P-47s to follow my lead for a strafe and bomb. The two other wings, White, and Blue, with four planes each would continue their nearby reconnaissance. We'd make a low pass as usual, strafing all the way from caboose to engine to shake them up, giving us time to circle around for a bomb run. I'd go in low and drop a five-hundred-pound bomb on the caboose, while Lewis, following close behind, would lob another one on the engine. The resultant craters and mangled tracks would cripple the train so we could circle around one more time and finish them off at our leisure. That was our standard M.O., and I must say we were very destructive that way.

• • •

We took off at 11:15 that morning from our hastily built airfield near Ophoven, Belgium, just north of Luxembourg, as our heavy P-47 Thunderbolts were only good for around three hours of combat flying. Our main mission was to maintain close air support for General Patton's Third Army, so we had to keep up with his rapid advance. Like checkers on a board, our squadron moved from one airfield to the next to stay within operational range. He was a hard man to keep up with.

One of our objectives that morning was to look for targets of opportunity. Forty-five minutes out, two of our wings glide-bombed a German bridge west of Cologne using eight- and eleven-second delayed explosives. The result was two large cavities in the bridge and significantly damaged abutments. Next, our squadron of eleven P-47s reconnoitered the Seigg River area near Bonn, and went on to Duttenfield to strafe a train marshalling yard with numerous rows of freight cars. We took out about ten railroad cars. It was hard to give an exact number since another fly-around cost extra fuel and exposed us to further enemy fire.

Another objective was to find a certain freight train that our ground operations reported had emerged from a tunnel near the Rhine River. They said it was possibly a mistake by the Germans, but they weren't sure. At that point of the war, their transport trains were constantly under attack from the air, so they usually remained in tunnels or forests until dark. Trains were the fastest way to get supplies to their units in a war situation, which made them all the more valuable to us. Every train we took out denied critical supplies needed by the German army. The downside for us was the further inside Germany we pushed, the more dangerous their trains became. They often had heavy armaments designed to fend off aerial attack, but there it was, out of the tunnel in the clear, waiting for us.

• • •

To do any kind of damage required us to be very close to the target. We circled around and banked for a fast dive from fifteen thousand feet and leveled off at about five hundred yards from the train. As we approached from the rear, I peered through the gunsight, pressed my right thumb on the top of the stick, and released a burst from four of my eight fifty-caliber wing-mounted machine guns. The bright flashes in front of the canopy and staccato gun bursts would last only seconds before I'd pull up for another go. I had to make it count. Focusing on the fast-moving target, I quickly worked the rudder pedals to swing my P-47 left and right as I walked my bullets from one end of the train to the other. I watched numerous, satisfying eruptions as my shells blasted through steel and sent splintering wood flying from the boxcars. It was all good until two seconds into the pass when I got a big surprise. Up ahead, the sides of several boxcars dropped open, displaying rows of twenty- millimeter flak guns.

"Oh, shit! Flak train!" I shouted into my radio. "Watch out!"

I slammed the accelerator full forward, increased my prop pitch, and pulled back hard on the stick. We knew too well how much damage a twenty-millimeter flak shell was capable of doing, so we got the hell out of there as fast as possible. But we weren't fast enough.

Normally, in that situation the first plane has the best chance of getting out without being shot up, while the second one might take some enemy fire. The troops on that train were quick. They began firing almost before the sides were down. They obviously expected us.

I saw the flashes before I heard the cannons, like ten blacksmiths pounding on red hot horseshoes. Although I pulled away fast, before I could make any distance their shells smashed into my fuselage with lethal force. When my engine started coughing and sputtering, I pulled back even harder on the stick to get as high and far away as possible. I managed to reach five thousand feet, but the engine coughed and sputtered even more. I didn't know if could stay aloft much longer.

"I'm hit," I radioed to the others. "I'll need a couple of minutes."

Training and experience taught me to immediately run through the emergency procedures. I went through everything on the list as fast as possible, but the engine continued its death rattle. Judging from the sound, at least half of the eighteen cylinders were damaged. I lost more airspeed and would soon go into a stall. I went through the procedures a second time, but nothing worked. I tried to go higher to buy more time, but the engine couldn't handle the load. I switched on my radio again.

"I'm heading out," I said. "I don't know how bad it is."

"Roger, Mike. We got it," said Lewis.

I'd lost sight of the train but I was still in their line of fire. Then the engine got worse, and without sufficient rpms I began to lose altitude. I knew I'd either crash or get hit again. Either way I was going down.

Helplessness was an unfamiliar feeling for me. Throughout my life, I always found a way out of bad situations, no matter how difficult. But nothing I did up there worked. I was falling. Then my helplessness turned to frustration, and in a moment of desperation I sought the Man upstairs.

"I can't handle this. Help me!"

I don't know where the message came from, but suddenly,

somewhere in my brain the strong message was there. *"Check the fuel transfer pump again."*

The transfer pump was part of the emergency procedures, and I already checked it twice. But the voice persisted, so I reached to the floor on the left side of my seat and switched the lever from main tank to auxiliary tank. The engine coughed a few more times, and then revved up again. Not full throttle, but fast enough.

I can't describe the great emotion I felt when the renewed engine pulled me out of my dive. I knew I was hit in several places, and the damage to the engine was critical. When it got going again, I knew I'd probably make it back to the base. I managed to avoid crashing and it made me feel tremendous.

The battle with the train raged below me, and as squadron leader I knew I should be with them. This was a time I had to be more concerned about my plane than worrying about the other guys. It was their problem now and this was mine. I banked in the direction of the base, flying slow while maintaining around five thousand feet.

• • •

Code named Advanced Landing Ground Y-32, the Ophoven field was built by the 820th Engineer Aviation Battalion in December 1944. Our hastily built runway—if you could call it a runway—was a patchwork of pierced, steel planking about forty-two hundred feet long that made for rough takeoffs and landings. Until I landed that day with all the shell holes and a sick engine, I'd always complained about the stress that strip put on my landing gear. Not that day. When all three wheels were firmly on the ground, I thanked the engineers under my breath for their good work. I taxied to a parking area, shut down the engine, and looked to the sky. "Thank You," I said.

When I pulled the cowling back and removed the helmet from my sweaty head, the crew chief trotted up. He had a scowl on his face.

"What the hell have you done to my airplane?"

"I don't know," I said, "It must have been those nasty old men I met out there."

When I climbed from the cockpit and planted my feet on the round, I had to lean against the fuselage a moment until the dizziness passed. Fortunately, stress didn't have much effect on me until everything was over. When I looked around, I saw what the crew chief meant. At least fifty holes had splattered from one end of the plane to the other. Usually after the first few missions, pilots didn't bother to count flak or bullet holes in their planes, and I have to say I had a lot. Some of the twenty-millimeter shells may have bounced off and exploded, which explained the small flak holes all over the place. It never occurred to me that one or more those shells could easily have lodged in my body, but that just wasn't in the cards that day. I guess I would summarize the way I felt by saying, "Well, I made it back again."

That was my sixteenth mission. Although Patton was on the march toward Munich and Hitler appeared to be on the run, my role in the war was only beginning. But none of that was on my mind then. I was tired and ready for a beer.

Part I

THE BEGINNING

═1═

1921 - Warren, Pennsylvania

If you happened to be walking in front of the community hospital in Warren, Pennsylvania on that frosty morning of February 27, 1921, you might have heard me. It was nearly 7 a.m. when I entered the world, all red, wrinkled, and screaming. I was okay, except for one small problem, which I'll discuss later. That aside, it was a happy day for Charles and Mabel Spencer. I was a healthy seven-pound baby with everything intact. Two weeks later, they christened me Howard William, the second of what would eventually be four surviving siblings.

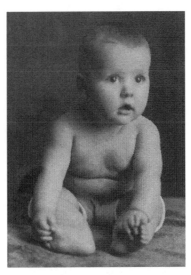

Howard (Mike), 1921

I grew up in a simple frame house on 129 Ford Street in Youngsville. It was a small borough in northwestern Pennsylvania, about fifty miles southeast of Lake Erie, and 175 miles due north of Pittsburgh. Viewed from ten thousand feet, Youngsville was a gentle place, nestled in the Broken Straw Valley surrounded by vast maple forests and the Allegheny Mountains. As it would turn out, the area was a perfect place to explore as a young boy.

A lot was going on in our part of America that year. Exciting things like the first Miss America beauty pageant held in Atlantic City and the Sunbury town council's edict requiring all women's skirts to be at least four inches below the knee. Enough was enough after all. There was also good news for my hard-working parents: the cost of bread dropped to five cents a loaf for the first time since the end of World War I. On the national scene, the new Charlie Chapman movie, The Kid, was released in its glorious flickering black and white.

It was also the year of the first live radio broadcast of the World Series, when the Yankees beat the Giants three to nothing. Albert Einstein won the Nobel Prize for physics that year, and the Chinese Communist Party was formed. That was also the time Adolf Hitler was elected president of the National Socialist German Worker's Party—an event that would affect my entire generation. On the positive side, life expectancy back then was 54.1 years. *(Funny how things change; as of this writing I am pushing ninety-six, and counting.)*

The year 1921 was relatively peaceful. World War I was in our past, the American economy was growing, and the Great Depression was still below the horizon. Coming into the world at that time might explain why I'm so optimistic, but I can't be sure. It stayed that way through my formative years, and for that I give thanks to many people. Most of the credit however, goes to three individuals who collectively bestowed on me the belief that life is not only hard work; it is also interesting, creative, and fun. I'm talking about my two parents and in particular my grandfather, Alton Mead.

Alton Mead, far left

☰ 2 ☰

A SOLID FOUNDATION

Charles and Mabel Spencer had five children in all. Jean, the first child, died at age three from a serious case of colitis, an inflammation of the large intestine. *(It would be many years before I would fully understand what it's like to lose a child.)* My big brother, Bob, was next, followed by me. Like Jean, I also came down with colitis at birth, and my parents thought I also might not make it. I pulled through, though. My little sister, Helen, came next, followed by my baby brother, Dick. Throughout my childhood, I got along fairly well with my siblings. We didn't have many spats, and the younger ones knew enough to stay out of my way.

My parents, Charles and Mabel Spencer

• • •

My dad's ancestors originally settled in Vermont and later migrated to an area south of Jamestown, New York. Dad spent some of his early years there but grew up in the Spring Creek area of Pennsylvania, about fifty miles southeast of Lake Erie.

Mom's ancestors settled in Massachusetts in 1635 and eventually moved to a small village—unnamed at the time—about forty-five miles south of Lake Erie (on Route 79 today). The town was eventually named Meadville, after my ancestor, Joshua Mead, who apparently got itchy feet in his hometown and moved there. My mom's parents, Alton and Ida Mead, eventually settled in the town of Spring Creek, near Broken Straw Creek, a pleasant locale where I would spend many of my younger years.

My parents were typical rural, pre-Depression, post-World War I folks. Neither of them made it any further than the eighth grade because the only educational opportunity they had was a small, country school. Unless they were among the fortunate few who studied in the big city, eighth grade was all they could get. Nevertheless, if my parents were short on formal learning, they scored high in the practical applications of life which were just as important. Both of my parents were raised in the Methodist Church, but I later decided the denomination lacked a strong doctrine related to Christ, and eventually looked elsewhere for spiritual fulfillment.

My father owned a 1920 Chevrolet: not an elaborate one, but at least it was transportation and good enough for me to use when I was learning to drive.

Dad was kind of like his Chevy: not elaborate but steadfast and true. I considered him to be somewhat of a philosopher of everyday life. He knew about practical things and believed in high morality. He was a good man, and we frequently had long conversations about practical things. The conversations were mostly generalities, however: neither deep nor insightful. For example, once I told him I was thinking about getting a landscaping job down the street. After two minutes of silence he replied, "Yeah I think that'd be all right." Then he was quiet another minute. "Do you know what you're going to ask?" I said I didn't intend to ask, but thought I'd let the owner of the house decide. Several minutes later he said, "Well, you could do that for your first job, but after that I think you ought to push it a little bit." That's how our conversations usually went.

I don't know how he found that beautiful mother of mine, because she was a knockout. Mom was a very thoughtful, compassionate, encouraging woman. She also taught me how to take care of my clothes, and how to cook. Although none of my brothers or sisters had any interest in cooking, for some unknown reason I did—baking in particular. Whenever she was in the kitchen baking something, I was Johnny-on-the-spot because I got to lick the bowl afterward.

Every night, Mother cooked a substantial meal, which we ate together as a family gathered around the table. It was mostly farm-type food: a lot of beef, biscuits, gravy, and a few vegetables. Our Sunday meal was usually roast beef with mashed potatoes, gravy, and cauliflower or green beans.

Bob (left) and me at 2 years old, 1923

My parent's outlook on life went along with their practical, hard-working existence. They weren't the gushy types, and they never went overboard with their emotions. They did remember birthdays, anniversaries and graduations, however, and there was usually a cake for these special occasions. Aside from those celebrations, our lives were very simple.

PARTY LINE

My dad's father, Jay Spencer, was a rural writer of minimal notoriety who penned articles benefitting the many farmers of our area. We got along well enough, but it was my grandfather on my mother's side—Alton Mead—who had a huge impact on my life. In my younger years, I spent a lot of time on his farm, mostly because Grandpa Alty apparently singled me out as the recipient of his personal mentoring. His life was different from ours: he lived in a very rural area while we lived in a small town. On days when we sat at dinner around Grandpa and Grandma Mead's great oak table, he'd tell us about life on the farm—fascinating things about nature, animals, and especially their unique telephone homeopathic medicine network.

Alton Meade Farm

In those days, if someone wanted to place a telephone call, they rang up the local switchboard operator, who connected the caller by placing a plug into the appropriate jack. That action allowed everyone else on the "party line"—which could allow up to twenty families within a seven-mile radius—to hear the conversation.

The way to know if the call was for you was to listen to the sound of the distinguishing beeps, but none of the conversations were private. Grandpa's house got two short tones and one longer one—*beep beep-beeeeep*, which sounded to me like the squealing wheels on a trolley car. If my grandmother heard *daah beep beep beep beep*, while knitting in her rocker, she knew the call was for the Dembowski's home several miles away. She'd go to the phone hanging on the wall next to the kitchen, quietly put the receiver to her ear, and listen in on the entire conversation. I can surmise that the party line had something to do with teaching Americans to be careful about what they said in public.

When someone got sick or had an accident, the whole community knew about it thanks to the party line. Depending on the ailment, such eavesdropping might galvanize the entire community to action. Everyone with an opinion pitched in with sage advice about this herbal remedy for the flu, that method of eliminating warts, or the best way to cure bee stings. No one could google Doctors.com back then, and precious few had access to a medical journal.

Most people in their area traveled around by horse and buggy, and if a health emergency arose, it could take hours for the doctor to arrive. With the party line, symptoms were quickly diagnosed and cures prescribed. Everyone put in their own two cents. Mary Simpson, down the road, gave sage advice, as did the Yeargins, who owned the big, red barn, and Alex Plimpton, the wheat farmer who had an entire wall filled with books. When the doctor finally arrived, his diagnosis and remedy might not be as quick or effective as what friends and neighbors had already provided. What the party line provided in terms of reassurance often made up for their incorrect diagnoses. As far as Grandpa Alty knew, no one died as a result of the party line.

While countless books would eventually come out about homeopathic medicine, the farming community around Youngsville actually practiced it. When my dad came down with diphtheria and my family was quarantined in our house, my grandparent's party line provided abundant goodwill and advice.

≡ 3 ≡

DREAMING

There were no kindergartens in Youngsville, so when I was six years old, I entered the first grade. Beginning with that first day of school, my overall learning experience was positive, even if I didn't have such a great time in my school's rare extracurricular activities. In the spring of that year, my Grandpa Jay stayed with us for a while to help during the quarantine from Dad's diphtheria. One spring day, when I must have had ants in my pants from cabin fever, Grandpa took me for a walk. He pointed out the budding trees, the greening fields, and various wildflowers popping up from between the rocks. He also spoke to me about life. I suppose he realized I needed some guidance at the time, or maybe he just liked me because I was curious about many things.

My likes, dislikes, and capabilities were all normal, judging from my peers, except that I didn't go out for school sports because my stature and weight were below the norm. I was a late bloomer. As I progressed through school, I helped out on Grandpa's farm, mostly during spring breaks and summer vacations. Whenever he could, he took me aside and taught me things about hunting and the ways of animals, trees, and life in general. His love of nature taught me to ask questions and led me into a life of curiosity and learning. Through those formative years, Grandpa had a large influence on my life, and I admired him greatly. *(I have to say that even today I still miss him very much.)*

When I was fourteen, I often hiked out to a field by the woods and lay on my back watching the clouds. I imagined how wonderful it would be to climb onto one of those big white puffs and just drift across the sky. I hoped to get up there some day, but I didn't know exactly how, since I was just a Pennsylvania farm boy. I couldn't know it at the time, but gazing beyond the horizon like that was an important first step in my future development.

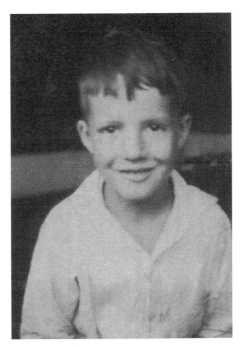

Me at age 5, 1926

4

MY MENTOR

One fall day before the frost set in, Grandpa showed me how beavers build their dams. "They're the world's second-largest rodent," he whispered as we crept up to the stream on all fours. "They build a dam to create a pool of deep water for protection and also to float sticks and limbs used to build their lodge. That's much easier than hauling them across the ground." He told me a lodge was their home, and when I looked through the bushes, I saw it, just ahead in the middle of a fast-flowing stream. It must have been ten feet wide and dome-shaped, like an igloo with only the top visible.

"Be real quiet, Howdy, because they're very conscious of anything coming toward them." *(He called me Howdy, but I can't recall how I got that nickname.)* They were building their house with all sorts of jumbled up twigs and branches, including a few logs as big around as a fencepost.

"Lift your head only a little, but don't move," whispered Grandpa. "If they spot you, they'll slap their big tails on the water to warn the others. And they're real loud." I tried to breathe as quietly as possible, although my heart was pounding.

I watched two beavers swim upriver pushing a big log that must have been six inches in diameter and about five feet long. I was amazed at the power those little guys had. Grandpa told me they probably chopped it down during the summer for later use, like stashing a pile of firewood for the winter. Apparently, they chew a circle around the base of the tree and keep chewing until it falls down. Then they trim the limbs off.

Grandpa said a beaver dam is built in such a way that if there's a heavy rainfall and the river floods, the dam won't wash away. The clever beavers engineer a kind of flow-through system to ease the pressure. If there is any damage, they just patch it up with mud and leaves. Later when winter sets in, the mud and water freezes until it's as hard as bricks. This was all very remarkable to me.

Age 13, 1934

• • •

One day in late summer, Grandpa and I hiked to an area where he thought bees might live. He told me he planned to get the honey and wax from the inside the tree. He said the most interesting part was finding out where the bees lived. When he found a good spot, he placed a pie pan filled with a mixture of water and sugar and placed it on a tree stump. "Stand way back, and be patient," he said. "Just watch."

Soon several bees hovered above the pan and settled on the edges.

"Now," whispered Grandpa, "watch to see where they go; they'll lead us right to the honeycomb."

After they ingested some of the sugar water, the bees all flew in the direction of a large, hollow, beech tree about a hundred yards away. There were many trees around, but they all went to that particular one.

"That's it," he said. "That's our treasure chest."

He pulled out a white piece of cloth, tied it around the beech, and we hiked back home. A couple of weeks later he told me it was time to get our honeycomb. We found the tree with the cloth still attached, gathered some firewood, piled it near the base of the tree, and lit it. When it reached a full blaze, Grandpa tossed wads of moist, green grass on top of the fire until it began to smoke. The gray plume curled up and around the hollow tree like a chimney, until several bees emerged from their hive and flew away. Once all the bees had flown away, Grandpa picked up his long crosscut saw.

"You take one end, and I'll take the other. We're gonna cut this thing down."

The tree was twice the size of a telephone pole, but we kept pushing and pulling that saw until my arms felt like they'd fall off. Finally the half-dead tree toppled and smashed to the ground, breaking into several chunks with the impact. We cut the trunk into pieces with the saw and used an axe to hack the rest of the way to the honeycomb. When it was exposed, I couldn't believe how much was there. We filled *eight* ten-gallon milk cans with the honeycomb! It was mostly wax of course, but there was still a lot of honey inside.

We hauled the cans to a cart and pulled the entire load back to the farm, where Grandma processed the combs. She put them in sacks and hung them above an oven with a low heat until the wax melted and the honey dripped into pans below. Hours later, we had dozens of jars of pure, forest-fresh honey.

5

MODERN TOM SAWYERS

Then there was the time a bunch of us guys in Youngsville got together and did something fairly unique. One Saturday in March 1935, when I was fourteen, we decided to take a joy ride on an ice floe. It seemed like a good idea at the time.

The setting was a small tributary of the Allegheny River that flowed through the middle of our town. Years earlier, engineers had created a bypass around the main bridge to reduce the damage caused by floating ice chunks during the spring floods. The widened portion of the river was about one and one-half feet deep, but the narrower bypass area was eight or ten feet deep and flowed faster than the rest of the river. As we stood around the river looking at the ice break away from the bank, someone said, "Hey, why not get on that ice and go someplace?" Since no one was smart enough to point out a good reason not to, the next Saturday about thirty guys—all teenagers—showed up at the bridge.

Somehow we organized a team to select the right floe and figure out how to get it to break away. By prior arrangement, most of us brought their dad's axes and their mom's clothesline poles, all the equipment we needed. *(I wonder what people would think today if they saw a gang of teenagers armed with axes and poles.)*

We walked along the riverbank, where remaining slabs of ice clung to the grass and earth. Larger chunks had broken off and slowly eased their way into the main flow. At one point, we came across a particularly large chunk that looked like it was about to break free. "Hey, that's the one!" a few yelled excitedly. Everybody gathered along the edge and began chopping away with axes and pushing with poles. "Come on. Go! Go!" It was a massive, iceberg-sized chunk at least a hundred yards long and thirty yards wide, and it didn't budge. Like a road gang, we kept hacking away. Then one of the big kids coordinated the effort and told us to focus on one spot on the upriver section of the ice.

"This is it, now push!" We all grunted and gave it our best shot. Sure enough, the ice began to break away, and we all cheered. It was quite a sight to watch that big, white platform, the size of a small parking lot, slowly move away. But as it broke free, it began to break up under its own weight. We watched several jagged cracks traverse its face until it separated into three roughly equal chunks. "Let's go!" someone shouted. We split up and scrambled onto the separate pieces, slipping and falling as we went, leaving the axes on the bank but keeping our poles. Soon, reminiscent of those fur-trading keelboats of the old West, we stood on the edge of our respective vessels and poled our way out to the middle.

Once we entered the main current of the river, I knew our voyage would be cut short. About a half mile past the town center, the river narrowed into rapids—not serious ones since it was still winter—but enough to expose us to rocks and eddies. Before we even got to the rapids, our piece with six guys began to split in half. Four of the guys stayed on the bigger chunk, while my friend Dan and I stuck with the smaller one, balancing precariously on a twenty-by-thirty-foot ice cube moving ever faster as it approached the rapids. Now that was exciting!

We cruised along at a good clip at about eight miles per hour, relaxing on our poles and watching the town drift by. A few people stopped to watch us with curiosity, but no one panicked. And there were no squad cars screaming up to tell us we broke some law. We felt absolutely free until one of us mentioned we should get off before we went too far. The ice had already broken up twice, and it would probably happen again.

We waited until the river flattened out somewhat and tried to pole close to an area by an old-folk's home. We pushed hard, but the current wouldn't let us get close enough. Our iceberg drifted past the home and out to the middle again, and now I began to get a little concerned. We poled harder to reach some part of the shore, and when that didn't work, Dan put down his pole and turned to me and shook his head.

"We aren't gonna get to the shore."

"All right," I said, "then we'll have to jump." I looked down at the water. "It's cold. Can you swim with your heavy clothes on?"

"Yeah," he said, "I think so."

Dan was a couple of years older than me, so I took his age as a barometer of wisdom. We slowly lowered ourselves over the edge, keeping our heads above water, and dog-paddled toward the shore. My wet clothing dragged like dead weight, so I had to paddle twice as hard as usual to make headway. When we made the shore, we stood up to watch our ice boat continue its journey for a couple of minutes, until I felt the chill reach my bones.

"Hey, my house is a mile or so up that way," I said, pointing to the area that cut across the woods. "Let's go." We had to move fast in that twenty-five-degree air … wearing soaked clothing increased the probability of hypothermia, although I didn't know what *hypothermia* meant at the time. I just knew I had to get to a warm place fast. As we trotted I remembered what Grandpa said about keeping active in freezing situations. We ran, shuffled, and walked, until we got to our respective homes. Mom heard me slam the door.

"Where have you been?" she asked.

"Oh, just riding an iceberg down the river."

"Well, of course you have," she said, eyeing crusts of ice clinging to my pants. I knew she didn't believe me.

"No, really, Mom. A bunch of us did." I explained our adventure through chattering teeth and finished with, "So I'm pretty frozen at the moment."

"Oh, okay then," she said with a look of concern. "Get out of those clothes and take a hot bath. What would you like for lunch?"

And that's how it went. No drama. No scolding. Aren't moms wonderful?

A couple of days later I heard that everyone in the ice adventure came out fine. As far as I know, no one since then has tried to ride ice floes down our river, or any other that I know of. That's how it was in my home town.

Age 16, 1937

CLAY COOKING

Occasionally, on an early Friday afternoon after school, I'd take off into the woods for an overnight trip. I took my backpack with a few essentials like a blanket, a flashlight, some wax-covered matches, a little salt, and bug spray. Then I'd grab my .22 rifle and call my faithful dog, Laddie. He was a beautiful mixed-breed dog, easily trained and obedient, doing everything a great dog should do. We'd head out of our yard and walk three blocks to the railroad tracks. We followed them a couple of miles, until we were deep in the forest, and then head into the thickest part of the woods. An hour or so later I'd find a good spot to camp, always near a creek for water and washing. We'd stay out there for a night, maybe two, just Laddie and I.

I remember one particular trip that makes my mouth water every time I think of it. After I set up camp, we immediately took off to find dinner. I knew I'd shoot something because I counted on Laddie, my partner and fellow hunter, who could see or smell things I never could. When he spotted something, he gave a muted, half-bark, just enough to get my attention. If I didn't pay attention, he'd yank my shirttail with his teeth until I stopped to look around. "Okay, boy, I see it!" Sure enough, there was a squirrel half way up a tree twitching its tail. I raised my rifle and got it on the first shot. I had to make it count since those little guys were quick. After I bagged a couple of squirrels, Laddie and I took a break on the soft needles of a pine grove to enjoy the silent sanctuary of the forest.

Back at our campsite, I skinned and gutted the squirrels and hung them from a tree close to where we camped. I hung them high so other animals wouldn't help themselves to our dinner. By then it was late afternoon … time to find our main meal for the next day. We hiked back into the forest until I found a tree that looked about right for what I wanted.

"Okay, boy, sit, and be real quiet," I whispered. Laddie crouched on his haunches without making a noise. I squatted against a rock and kept my .22 at the ready. As we waited, I played a little game with my dog. If I raised my rifle just a little, Laddie's ears twitched as if to say, "I'm going to get something." When I lowered it, his ears dropped back down. He was always in the middle of the game with me.

The tree was a mid-sized pine about fifteen feet tall with lots of branches. By then—I was fifteen—I knew what grouse did around that time of the day and in what kind of tree they usually nested. With my rifle aimed toward the top of the tree, we waited in silence.

Sure enough, two large grouse flew in, landed, and set about doing whatever grouse do before turning in for the night. It would be a while before they went to sleep, so Laddie watched me watch them without making a peep. Twenty or so minutes later, their movements began to slow, and with that I knew I was about to get a shot. While a .22 isn't the most powerful rifle, at only fifteen feet away I had no doubt it would bring down a grouse. I slowly aligned the muzzle, took careful aim at the larger of the two grouse, and fired.

It toppled down out of the tree and landed a few feet from Laddie, who became very excited. He ran back and forth between the grouse and me until I said, "Okay, boy, pick it up." He gently clenched the lifeless bird between his jaws and happily trotted by my side back to our campsite.

It was a male—about twice the size of a female—so it would be a good meal. I cut his head off, gutted him, removed his legs, and washed what remained in the stream. Then I hung it high at the end of a thin tree branch. A thin branch would break easily, and animals knew better than to climb too far out on it. We cooked and ate one of the squirrels that night; it was scant eating but enough to keep me going until the big meal the next day. I slept on my blanket atop a pile of pine boughs.

Early the next morning I checked to see if the grouse carcass was still there. It was. I washed it in the creek again and stuffed the cavity with wet, green grass I collected near the water. Next I scooped up several handfuls of clean, thick mud from the creek bank and pasted it all over the bird—feathers and all—until it was caked with about three inches of mud. The result was a big, wet mass about the size of a basketball. Then I built a big fire.

I barbecued the remaining two squirrels on a spit: one for me and one for Laddie. When we finished, I piled several more pine logs on the fire and lowered the mud basketball into the center of the coals. Then I piled more wood on top. With my grouse in the oven, we set out to explore the forest for a few hours. Since this was only a one-night trip, it wasn't necessary to hunt more squirrels, so we just hiked around.

When we returned to the campsite around two in the afternoon, the fire was out but still warm. Gray ashes outlined the blackened clay basketball that was hard as a rock. I lifted it out, placed it on a bed of pine needles, and gave it several whacks with the butt of my rifle. It split open, revealing a fully-cooked, naked and steaming bird. Its feathers had separated from the skin and stuck to the walls of the clay while it cooked. What I held in my hand was over three pounds of freshly cooked game. Laddie danced around my feet, salivating.

After I built the fire up again, I skewered the bird on a shaved, green spruce branch and held it over the flames to warm it up. When it had browned on the outside, I added a little of my salt, and we proceeded to feast. There I was, leaning against a log near the campfire by a small creek in the middle of the woods with my dog at my side eating freshly cooked grouse. There was no finer experience in my memory, and no better feeling, than what I felt that afternoon. If my life had stopped at that very moment, I would have left the world altogether content, wanting nothing.

MAPLE SYRUP

As I got older, I continued to help around Grandpa Alty's farm. I hauled hay in the summer, did various odd jobs around the house or barn, and picked apples in the fall. One of my more memorable jobs was harvesting syrup from his sugar maple grove, which I did every April until I finished high school.

Grandpa said the spring harvest actually begins in late fall, when the trees begin to lose their leaves. As it grows colder, the sap withdraws into the roots at the same time the leaves turn color, die, and start to fall off. The trees hibernate throughout the winter until early spring, when the sun grows warmer. Then the spring rains come, allowing the roots to absorb water. The water, which contains the maple sugar, in turn makes its way up from the roots to the limbs to feed the new buds.

"That's when harvest time is about right," said Grandpa one morning on his front porch. "The bark of that tree is like a blood vessel. It ain't the wood that feeds 'em, it's the bark, and we've got about two weeks to get that sap while it's still flowin'."

We'd drill a hole through the bark and insert a tube about the size of Grandpa's bony finger, placing it at an angle to let the sap flow downward. Then we hung a four-gallon pail below the little tap. Depending on its size and health, a tree with two taps gave up to twenty gallons of sap every day. Each afternoon, we went through the grove with a big tank drawn by two horses to empty the buckets. If there was still snow on the ground, we'd pull the container on a sled— hard work when we had to tug it uphill to Grandpa's maple shack.

Inside the smoky shack were iron stands, a fire pit, a chimney, and three big pans stacked one on top of the other. My job was to keep the fire lit while the sap cooked. As the sap heated up and got thicker, it ran from the top pan, down to the next pan, and then to the bottom one. We kept the fires going twenty-four hours per day for two or more days until the job was done. Grandpa had another hired hand to help, but he held me accountable for those fires. To make sure, I camped out on the floor between two blankets near the fire, waking up throughout the night to stoke the flames. As the sap—with the consistency of sugar water—boiled down, the original fifty gallons of sap reduced to about one gallon of syrup. That's why the real stuff is so expensive.

. . .

Washing Post Office windows, 1938

I was always busy during the school years and on summer breaks. Aside from helping Grandpa Jay, I did other odd jobs, because we didn't get allowances as kids. I washed windows, mowed lawns, and worked in gardens. Like most families with limited income, I wore hand-me-down clothes, including my big brother's knickers—the kind that hung just below the knees. I remember my first long pair of pants, given to me before I graduated from junior high school. My mother said I could have a regular pair of trousers as long as I took care of them. I told her she had a deal, so she taught how to use the iron. That's how I learned how to take care of my own clothes.

• • •

The times with Grandpa were fun and educational, and I believe they also prepared me to deal with difficult, even life-threatening situations. One cold winter day when I was thirteen and out bear hunting deep in the forest with two older friends, I became separated from them. Apparently I got carried away following some tracks, and when I looked up, my friends were gone. All I had was my rifle and a light jacket. I called out for my friends quite a few times but got no response. It was dead silence. I had no idea which way they had gone. As the afternoon wore on, the temperature dropped to the low thirties. I was tired, so I sat down at the base of a tree and waited. That's when it got dangerous.

I could have easily fallen asleep, but I remembered Grandpa telling me one time when we were out hiking that the worst thing I could do if I was tired and cold was to go to sleep. He said I had to fight sleep with all I had and to be sure to keep moving. His words were still clear in my memory, so I got up and started walking. Finally when it was almost dark, I spotted a group of trees near a clearing and remembered the rest of the way back home.

⹀ 6 ⹀

STRETCHING UP AND OUT

I didn't hang around with a bunch of guys during my middle school years. My best friend and schoolmate was Alton Proper, and we went hunting together or went on overnight camping trips in the woods. When I was eleven, I ran briefly with a local gang of sorts. There were six of us who, like me, needed encouragement from a bunch of guys experiencing the same strange, sometimes difficult stage of life. We didn't do much except make a lot of noise and steal corncobs to throw at each other …, which wouldn't qualify for delinquency even now. When I wasn't out running with the gang, I had my faithful dog Laddie.

By the end of junior high, I was barely five feet tall and only weighed one hundred pounds, even after eating a big meal. My size was disappointing to me because I didn't feel comfortable playing basketball or football like the rest of the guys, and our school didn't have any track and field activities. My biggest fear at the time was that I might go through life as a midget. To make up for my size deficiency, I developed my own kind of extracurricular activities that usually involved being outdoors. It often involved hunting of some kind.

I used a lightweight .410 shotgun for hunting birds and squirrels, if I could get close enough. I sometimes liked to fish, but it never became an obsession. When I caught a bass or a trout, I'd build a fire next to the stream, cook it, and eat it on the spot. I never caught a fish just to throw it back, because in my estimation the idea of hunting is to eat what you catch. I didn't understand the "catch-and-release" business.

My gang life came to an end when I joined the Boy Scouts. Our local troop kept me interested in outdoor things while providing for some of my social needs. We camped out a lot, hunted, fished, and learned about animals and how they behaved in the wilderness. I attended a 1936 International Boy Scout Jamboree in Washington, DC. That really impressed me: I loved the city and thrived on the exposure to Scouts from other countries.

After graduating from junior high school, I worked with an ice-cream company as a delivery boy. Delivering all that ice cream and running around must have helped me grow, because by the end of summer, I'd added two sorely-needed inches to my height and gained twenty-two pounds. It was a relief to be somewhat normal in size, knowing I wouldn't have to go through life as a midget.

I took up tennis in my junior year in high school and actually became pretty good at it. After I got my driver's license, I also got a job as a chauffeur for a bank examiner from Jamestown named Charlie Miller. I drove him from meeting to meeting or back to his home at the end of the day. One afternoon when he came out of a particularly long meeting, he asked me what I planned to do after I graduated. I told him my dad didn't earn much money as a bank clerk, so I wasn't' sure what I would do. I clearly remember his response:

"Well, we can't allow that to happen."

We talked a little more and he said, "There's an accounting school in Boston named Bentley, and you might want to think about going there. It's less expensive than other colleges."

I thought about it, but didn't know how I could afford to go there since it was probably expensive, but when an opportunity arose later, it would change my life.

Throughout my school years, I never had what I'd call a steady girlfriend. I think I was somewhat shy, still exploring my world and trying to grow up. Occasionally I'd find a girl to go out with, and I always managed to find one to go with me to the prom. If not, sometimes she found me.

Age 18, 1939

• • •

I came into my own during senior high, a period when I morphed from a loner to a joiner. I enjoyed all aspects of study, particularly history. I took up the trumpet and played fairly well for the high-school band. I also played drums for the American Legion Drum and Bugle Corps. Neither of my parents had pushed me to take up an instrument, but when I did, they never discouraged me. I also joined the school's debate team. The discipline required to prepare for and win a debate forced me to dig deep into research. The result was a keen appreciation for the learning process. I also took three years of Latin, which helped me articulate in a debate. It also boosted my vocabulary and helped lay a foundation for acquiring other foreign languages. In my freshman year, I was elected class president. Apparently they liked the job I did, because they reelected me the following three years. When I wasn't playing instruments, studying, debating, and serving as class president, I worked at various odd jobs to earn spending money.

One day I built a portable shoeshine box. I planned to take it to the center of town where businessmen wore the kind of shoes that needed to be polished. When my dad saw what I was up to, he asked in his usual thoughtful way:

"Well, ya know it's a little unusual … people might make comments." He thought a minute. "Will that bother you?"

"No, I need some spending money."

He didn't say anything further.

As it turned out, I found my best customers in the pool hall, a place my parents would not have approved of if they had known where I was. Between shoeshine clients, I learned how to shoot pool. After a while, I got pretty good at it and earned even more money winning competitions. The extra cash from my pool winnings and my magazine delivery job definitely helped my social life. Now I could afford to take a girl out on a proper date.

• • •

I graduated from high school in 1939 with top grades and wore the sash of magna cum laude during commencement. It was interesting that the guy who made summa cum laude beat me by a mere .01 percent GPA. With that behind me, I was more than ready for the next step because a couple of years earlier I already knew I didn't want to stay in Youngsville. I enjoyed my life there, but it wouldn't be long until there was nothing more to interest me.

That was also the year Franklin Roosevelt won his second term as president. His New Deal seemed to be taking hold when the Great Depression was at its deepest. Adhering to the popular notion of isolationism brought on by the horrors of World War I, Roosevelt focused on taking care of the third of the American population who were "ill-housed, ill-clad, and ill-nourished."

Meanwhile, Germany simmered with social unrest: there was a cultural revolution that began in 1931, when Adolf Hitler emerged as Germany's strong leader. Germans wanted change, and Hitler promised he would deliver.

Part II

THE TRAINING YEARS

January, 1942 – June, 1944

☰ 1 ☰

EVERYTHING CHANGED

I moved closer to the group huddled around the radio so I could hear the announcer. His words were clipped, his voice, strained.

> "From the NBC News room in New York …
> President Roosevelt said in a statement
> today that the Japanese have attacked
> Pearl Harbor in Hawaii … from the air.
> I repeat that … President Roosevelt
> said that the Japanese have attacked
> Pearl Harbor in Hawaii from the air …
> this bulletin came to you from the NBC
> newsroom in New York."

It was shortly after 2 p.m. on December 7, 1941. A friend and I had just emerged from a theater in Sharon, Pennsylvania, after seeing *The Maltese Falcon* with Humphrey Bogart and Peter Lorre. All of Pennsylvania was crazy about the film. Once outside in the sunny afternoon, I could tell something was wrong. I could almost feel a certain buzz, an intensity in those around me. No one smiled. They hurried back and forth or talked animatedly among themselves on the sidewalk. Then I saw a group of people in the coffee shop next door listening intently to the radio on a shelf above the counter. When we went in, we heard the announcement about the Japanese attack on our navy fleet in Pearl Harbor. The siege had lasted a full hour and a half, and it was already over by the time I heard the newscast.

• • •

Years before, after I graduated from high school, I decided to take the advice of my bank examiner boss and attend the Bentley school of Accounting and Finance in Boston. I'd talked to my dad about it, and he said, "Mike, I couldn't send your older brother to college because I couldn't afford it. But maybe there's something we can do." He didn't make much money, but he helped me get a small loan for tuition and expenses. I suppose because of his position at the bank, they couldn't turn him down. The bank made me a nine-thousand dollar loan, and at the age of eighteen I packed my bags and hopped a Greyhound bus for Boston.

Bentley was no Harvard, to say the least. It was a two-year financial institution for poor people to learn accounting, business law, taxes, and so forth. But it was still a good school, and it required a lot of work. All the instructors were CPAs who doled out mountains of homework every night, so there wasn't much time for socializing. By the time I graduated at age twenty in 1941, I felt I understood how the American economy operated.

Not long afterward, I landed a job with Westinghouse Corporation in a little town named Turtle Creek, in Pennsylvania, and wound up in their transformer division in Sharon, Pennsylvania. I didn't like the job very much; it required a lot of detail and didn't call for much thinking, which didn't suit my interests at all. I won't call it fate, but I was at a point in my life when I needed something different. I could not tolerate what appeared to me to be a dead-end job, particularly at my age. I stayed with Westinghouse for just over a year, mostly to firm up my employment background and grow my résumé. It was around that time when I walked out of that theater and heard the announcement about Pearl Harbor. It didn't take me long to decide what to do. I was twenty-one years old and ready for a change, so three weeks after the announcement, I enlisted in the army.

• • •

I wanted to be a pilot, but the United States Army Air Corps required all pilot trainees to have a college degree. Since my accounting diploma wasn't enough, I signed up as an aircraft mechanic so I could learn all about airplanes. I hoped that would be an avenue to become a pilot, to fulfill the dreams I had had years earlier as I was lying on my back in a field watching the clouds.

My hopes were dashed when the army sent me to Camp Lee, Virginia, right after my induction. It was their quartermaster training base. Apparently they found out that I had an accounting degree and thought I was better suited for distributing supplies and provisions to soldiers than working on airplanes. I immediately decided that wasn't going to be my career, so I started badgering everyone up and down the ranks to let me join the aviation cadet program. I kept it up for quite a while, until a door opened. As the war expanded, the army's need for aviators became critical, and they waived the requirement of a college degree.

As soon as I found out about this, I signed up for an aviation aptitude test and passed it. I was delighted when I said goodbye to my short-lived assignment of handing out sheets and laundry bags. I caught the earliest train to Santa Ana, California, where I was to attend the West Coast Air Corps Training School. By then, the reality of the war had affected everyone. Shortly after I arrived in Santa Ana, I wrote my parents.

January 15, 1942

Dear Mom and Dad;

Rationing must be quite the fashion this season, isn't it? At least you can still take a bath without a ration card, or can you? You will probably miss the Sunday drives we used to take, but from what I have read, the ban on pleasure driving is only temporary.

Love, Howard

FLIGHT SCHOOL

The West Coast Air Corps Training School was tantalizingly close to Hollywood, where heroes like Humphrey Bogart, John Wayne, and Ingrid Bergman lived and worked. There was such a big turnover of service personnel at the school that celebrities often put on shows for the base personnel. Unfortunately, I couldn't attend any of the shows: since I was new, they expected me to learn about flying and nothing else. The facility was for ground training only, so there were no planes, hangars, or runways. I wasn't disappointed, though. The facility offered basic courses in math, aircraft-engine mechanics, world geography, and weather—subjects that opened up a new world of study, which I loved.

We slept in tents on a field scraped bare of all that was green, which was a very unusual sight for a Pennsylvania farm boy. We wore flight coveralls except on days off, when we got to wear a uniform. The uniforms made us look like we were in the regular army, except for the silver airplanes pinned on each lapel and a large hat with an oversized pair of wings on the front. On our occasional days off, a few buddies and I went to a friend's house in Laguna Beach, about fifty-five miles from the base. Our friend Franklin's parent's lived a block away from the ocean, and that's where I was first introduced to surfing.

Me in California, 1942

We got up early, grabbed our boards, and paddled out past the surf line. With the help of my friends, I managed to keep my balance and actually caught a few waves. It was great fun, and we kept that up until late morning when the wind blew out the surf. Then we went back to their house to lounge around until it was time to get back to the field.

During our days at Laguna Beach, I made friends with a couple of guys who were character artists with Walt Disney. They were … two of the funniest people I've ever met. They took me fishing in their small boat a few times, and somehow there was always a problem. We either ran out of gas or broke down, so they had to call the coast guard for a tow. No matter what the problem, they always turned it into some kind of a party. My friends on the West Coast opened my eyes to another lifestyle I never would have experienced, had I stayed in Pennsylvania. The world was indeed rich, interesting, and fun, in spite of the war that raged across the water.

After ten weeks of preliminary flight training, they assigned me to an air base at Tulare, in the heart of California's Central Valley ..., a place where it never rains. Tulare was where J.G. "Tex" Rankin— the noted stunt pilot—secured a United States War Department contract to operate a civilian flight school for air corps cadets. In its heyday, Rankin Field trained over ten thousand pilots in its primary flight school. After it opened, West Coast spy hysteria prompted the army to take control of Tulare's county fairgrounds and convert it to the Tulare Assembly Center—a detention center for Japanese Americans during the war. I didn't know the implications of that program until much later. I only thought of Tulare as the place I finally learned to fly solo.

After many more hours of classroom instruction, we were introduced to a classic airplane called the Stearman, a biplane on which I had my first flying experience. The Stearman had become *the* primary trainer for the US Navy and the US Army Air Corps, and remained so for the duration of the war. Later, Stearmans would serve as crop dusters and stunt planes. When I first saw its twin wings and protruding circle of pistons behind the big prop, it reminded me of the old circus barnstorming planes flying from town to town putting on air shows. I immediately fell in love with it.

What made my Tulare experience even better was my civilian instructor, Frank, who'd racked up eight thousand hours in his career as a service pilot. Frank was about as good as I could expect, since today's commercial pilot is required to have only fifteen hundred hours before taking the left seat of a plane ferrying hundreds of passengers.

= 2 =

MY FIRST SOLO

I remember that day as clearly as this morning's breakfast. There was a blue, sunny sky with no wind. In other words, perfect for flying— which is the reason there were so many airfields in California and Arizona. Hardly any cloud cover to speak of. No rain. No storms. Nothing but heat. The only things interfering with flight were infrequent dust storms, and when they hit they were awful. They were like huge walls of gray-black, swirling dirt thousands of feet high and barreling across the desert toward our base. If it was uncomfortable for us, it was a nightmare for our mechanics, whose job it was to insure the fine sand and grit wouldn't impair the engines. All we could do was hunker down in the barracks or sit tight inside a vehicle until the storm was over.

Frank and I took off on a perfect day. As we climbed, the temperature dropped, as cool wind licked around the windshield and buffeted my face. We performed several practice flights that morning, conducting procedures from takeoff to landing. I killed the engine during flight and started it up again. Then I did several touch-and-go rounds. Once, when we stopped, Frank switched seats with me and sat in front, the place normally assigned to trainees.

On the next flight, he let me handle the controls most of the time. Once I got used to the controls, I felt more confident, mainly because he was right in front of me. That went on until noontime, when we brought the plane in and taxied up to the hangar. With the engine still running, Frank turned around, grinning.

"Lunch can wait," he shouted over the engine. "You stay in the cockpit."

I gave him an inquisitive look, but he held up his hand.

"Your turn. Go ahead; take it up for a while."

The knot in my stomach tightened as I wondered if I really could fly that thing by myself. I knew that moment would come eventually, but this was too soon.

"Okay," I shouted, putting on a brave face.

He climbed out and stood in the shade of the hangar while I taxied to the end of the runway, pivoted, and took a deep breath. I gave it full throttle and roared down the runway. At first I overcompensated on the stick, resulting in the two front wheels tap-dancing on the left and then on the right. Somehow I managed to get it off the ground. Heading straight and climbing steadily, I looked behind as the airstrip grew smaller. I couldn't see Frank, but I felt his eyes boring into my back. I wasn't about to let him down.

At five thousand feet up, my knees stopped knocking, and I began to relax. The plane responded well, as I eased the stick forward, then back. Left, then right. Now I understood how a seagull must feel: soaring, gliding, and banking. Up there I could go anywhere and do anything I wanted. I experienced free, uninhibited flight for the first time, and I could hardly contain my excitement. I got a little creative, more for my benefit than Frank's, who I'm sure kept watching me from the ground. I managed to pull off a few simple rolls, making sure they weren't too difficult. I must have played around up there for at least an hour. When I made my not-so-perfect landing and taxied to the hangar, Frank stood there, beaming and applauding.

I found the Stearman a little hard to fly at first, probably because it was my first airplane. After I got used to it, though, I found it was a great plane for aerobatics and did just about anything I asked. I could pull a snap roll and a barrel roll. I performed loops and learned how to stall and how to recover from a stall.

In the process of learning to fly, I also learned a few things about myself. I was careful in the cockpit, not prone to extreme hotdogging stunts, although later I would learn how to push the envelope in other ways. I couldn't imagine doing things beyond what I knew the plane or I could handle. In many respects, this conservative, methodical approach to flying would later influence my professional life. By the time I finished basic flight training at Tulare, I had about one hundred flying hours under my belt.

• • •

Our next stop was Lemoore, California, an army-air force training field about forty-five miles south of Fresno, hastily built after Pearl Harbor. All it had was an airfield, a PX gas station, cadet quarters, officer's quarters, a mess hall, and a fleet of Vultee P-66 Vanguards. The 6,500-foot hard-surface runway was designated by the army as "available only when dry," which wasn't a problem since it never rained there anyway.

We would train at least fifty hours at Lemoore in a Vultee, a twin-seat, single-wing fighter first produced in late 1940. The Vultee was more powerful than most planes of its type and had several characteristics not available in a Stearman, although I couldn't appreciate them at the time. I was not at all impressed by the Vultee's handling: it shook and rattled and wasn't very exciting to fly at all, nor did it perform aerobatics very well. It had a tendency to ground loop, a dangerous, involuntary spin on its wheels just after landing. Maybe I was spoiled, since I lost my virginity with the Stearman and had a special attachment to it. My time with the Vultee turned out to be short lived though. The war demanded new, better-designed fighters and stopped building Vultees in 1942. Regardless of my opinion of the Vultee (like those of several fellow cadets), we went on to graduate in good standing.

Then the powers that were sent us off to a base near Phoenix, Arizona, named Luke Field. Unlike Lemoore, Luke had an irrigations system, so a little green grass grew here and there, which was nice. There was no town nearby ... not that it would have mattered since we didn't get much time off anyway. When I was there, Luke was relatively unpopulated, but it would eventually become the largest fighter training base in the US Army Air Forces, graduating over seventeen thousand pilots during the war years.

We trained for ten weeks in the P-40 Warhawk fighter, another single-winged, single-seat fighter that would be the second-most-used plane after the P-47 and the one I was destined to fly in Europe. Unlike the Vultee though, the Warhawk handled better and was an altogether more satisfying plane to fly.

SOARING

Somewhere in the midst of all the regimentation, the hours of study, and the intense training, the unfettered joy of flight began to fill my soul. Flying was far more than what I imagined as a boy lying on my back in the field behind my grandfather's farm. I discovered that, like any man, when he climbed into the cockpit and rose from Earth— whether in a glider, a balloon, or an airplane—he left everything behind and became completely free. Up there I was of something different, as if I were magically transformed into another shape or being. Hurtling through the air at three or four hundred miles per hour with no restriction on movement gave me a thrill I cannot explain. If I wanted to do something up there, I just did it. There was no car behind me, no people in my way, and no one to tell me I was dreaming. I could roll over, take a sharp turn, do a snap roll, or play hide and seek with the clouds. I just did what I wanted to do.

In the air, I controlled my plane in three dimensions instead of only two on the ground. When I finally came back to Earth and landed, I felt a kind of exultation mixed with exhaustion, partly from the adrenalin rush and partly because flying takes a lot of conscious effort. Skills gained from tracking bears in the woods or solving difficult accounting problems conditioned me to be 100 percent attentive in the cockpit. Discipline and focus aside, the exultation of soaring thousands of feet above the Earth was unparalleled by anything I'd ever experienced before. I couldn't express the feeling better than the first man who flew across the Atlantic Ocean alone:

> *"Sometimes, flying feels too godlike to be attained by man.*
> *Sometimes the world from above seems too beautiful, too*
> *wonderful, and too distant for human eyes to see."*
> — *Charles A. Lindbergh*

The fascination of flight is forever. Now that I'd experienced it, I would never be able to forget it.

First Solo Flight in 1942

⚌ 3 ⚌

GRADUATION

The big day came on December 3, 1942, when we became officers, gentlemen, and pilots all at once. Not surprisingly, our group was destined to fight in the skies of the Pacific or Europe, depending on the immediate need, which was the reason we signed up for flight training in the first place. The day after the graduation, several of us received the most disappointing news imaginable. They assigned us to be flight instructors. Apparently, our war manufacturing industry turned out more airplanes than there were pilots, so the Army Air Corps ramped up the training program. Suddenly, and without any combat experience whatsoever, we were supposed to tell somebody else how to fly a fighter plane in a war zone. I was a new second lieutenant, and although very proud to pin my new gold bar on my lapel, the news took away my joy.

In the early months of 1942, Japanese troops had penetrated the defenses of Malaysia and advanced into Borneo. Right after declaring war on the Netherlands, they invaded the Dutch East Indies and took twenty-five thousand soldiers prisoner, mostly British. Next, they conquered Singapore. The good news was the US naval victory at the Battle of Midway, which marked the turning point in the Pacific War. In Europe, Germany's march through Russia bogged down at Stalingrad, and the mass incarceration of Jewish people spread throughout all of Hitler's occupied countries. We followed the news closely, and the more we learned, the more eager we were to jump into the fight. But no, we had to stay behind to train new pilots so they could go instead of us.

Becoming an Officer, 1942

After a brief advanced instrument course in Sacramento, California, about eighty of us were assigned to the Army Air Forces Flight Training Command in Yuma, Arizona. Formerly known as Fly Field, the Yuma airfield consisted of two dirt runways converted for training use and activated in December 1942. If I thought Phoenix was hot, Yuma—with an average summer temperature of 107°F—beat all the records. Sometimes after I climbed into the plane and closed the canopy, the cockpit instantly became a 114°F greenhouse. Regardless of my disappointment and discomfort, I tried to keep my letters on the humorous side:

February 9, 1943

Dear Mom and Dad,

The sand is still eighteen inches deep, and the meals are still pretty awful. The blankets still scratch, and I'm constantly being switched from one squadron to another. It's very hot, yet I can't understand why I like it so much here in Yuma! Golly Mom, I'll bet you're the glamor girl of the town with your new coat and hat. Do you still go steady with Dad? It's good to hear you finally got a permanent set of teeth and had your glasses changed.

Love, Howard

The town of Yuma had nothing to offer, really. The population hovered around two thousand, and if we wanted a good steak, we had to cross the border to Mexico three hundred yards beyond the southwest boundary at Broad Street. On the upside however, I drank my first Corona Beer in Yuma, and to this day I remain highly thankful for the introduction. Still, that was little compensation for being stuck there while the war raged overseas. As I wrote my parents:

August 1943

Dear Mom and Dad,

Do you remember Tony Karahalios? I just received a letter from him. He is flying transport planes in Texas. He is quite disappointed but hopes to get across in a few months. When we were at Camp Lee together we used to stay up until 2 or 3 a.m. walking around and talking about how we would be fighter pilots in the same squadron. We must have spent four or five hours a day just talking and dreaming about when we would get our wings and be sent to combat. Right now I'd gladly trade my second lieutenant's rank for an assignment to single engine fighters..

Love, Howard

While I continued to gain valuable hours in the cockpit, I kept in touch with others already engaged in the "real war." I was sad when I read about a friend of mine who was one of the early casualties of the war not battling on the front lines:

October 1943

Dear Mom and Dad,

Dick Richards was killed in Alaska a few months ago in a navy plane. Mr. Bradley, of Bentley College, wrote a letter the other day telling me about it. Also, Leila said Claude Neely was a German prisoner-of-war. It makes one realize that there is a war going on..

Love, Howard

The longer I trained others for combat flying, the more I knew I was supposed to be "over there" doing what they trained me to do. By that time in my life, I realized I was a talker and could convince people to do things through lots of persuasive conversation. When my frustration reached the boiling point, I took action by starting what I called an "irritation program." I started to badger my superiors, the director of flight training, and anyone else who would listen. I told them I'd done a good job as an instructor, and now it was time to let me go and join the fight. I didn't get immediate results, but felt if I kept it up that someday, someone would pay attention and do something about it …, even if their only motivation was to shut me up.

THE DANCE

Meanwhile, somebody way above me decided to kick it up a notch and train B-17 crews for deployment to the war. We trained their entire crew: gunners, radio techs, pilots, and copilots. The B-17 was that big, four-engine "flying fortress" with machine gun pods protruding from its nose and tail. The Defense Department had recently upgraded the B-17, and our job was to train the crews with the most recent models. We'd fly the older models to a depot near Harrisburg, Pennsylvania, and return to Yuma with the new ones. Since all of us wanted to get out of Yuma in the worst way, most of us volunteered for delivery duty. Fortunately, I was selected on a number of occasions.

The B-17 didn't have enough fuel capacity to make the twenty-eight-hundred-mile trip between Yuma and Harrisburg, so we had to refuel somewhere along the way. That also required an overnight stop since that big, heavy bomber didn't fly very fast. At 250 miles per hour, we didn't make a lot of headway.

On one particular delivery in January 1943 my crew and I decided to make a fuel stop in Kansas City on our way to Pennsylvania. *(That was another thing I liked about being a pilot—we had significant latitude in our decision making.)* After we landed and secured the plane at the military end of the airport, my copilot and I found a nice hotel near the center of the city. We checked in and immediately went down to the lobby bar and, oh man, did our eyes bug out! All the guys had gone to war, and the place was packed with beautiful girls. My crew chimed in at once: "We go no further ... this is where we're spending the night."

I thought about it and said, "You know what I'd really like to do? I'd like to find someplace to dance." I didn't think I'd do much with those girls anyway, since I was pretty shy and conservative. Instead, I went out front and asked a taxi driver where I could find a dance hall.

"How would Tommy Dorsey do for ya?" he asked.

"That's exactly what I'm looking for," I said. "He's from my home state of Pennsylvania!"

I not only liked Dorsey, I liked the whole swing fad of the day and also liked Frank Sinatra. The cabbie dropped me off in front of the Cowtown Ballroom at the edge of the city. I already had supper, as most people ate before they went out in the evening in those days, so I was ready for my night out. I paid $1.50 for my ticket, went inside, and sat down on one of the seats along the edge of the dance floor. *(I was a lieutenant on flight pay so I could now afford it.)* Waiting on the sidelines, I asked myself what I was looking for. It looked like I could pick one of several attractive girls. I decided I wanted someone talkative, but not too much so. I wanted someone pretty too and who laughed a lot. I thought she should be having fun while she's dancing, not just going through the moves to get a date.

I watched couples move slowly around the room in a circular motion. That's how they did it in those days, just dance, spin, and rotate nice and easy like. Then I spotted one gal who seemed to be really enjoying herself. I waited for her to go around a couple of times and finally decided she was the one for me. She was a good dancer, and so was the guy with her. Being a farm boy from northern Pennsylvania didn't set me up to be a good dancer, although I'd done a little dancing in the past. Grandpa told me that's how he wooed Grandma at first, except they were square dancing. Well, I could square dance like the best of 'em, but I was not the greatest ballroom dancer. Anyway, when she finally sat down, none of the guys claimed her, so I decided to be the aggressor. I walked over to her and asked her for the next dance.

I checked my hat at the door when I came in, but my uniform made it obvious that I was an officer and a fighter pilot, and I intended to let her know it in case she hesitated to dance with me. When I asked her, she responded right away, though. "Yes, sure." So I didn't have to say anything more. We headed out to the floor when Dorsey began playing "On the Sunny Side of the Street."

We danced the first one—somewhat awkwardly in all honesty, —but when the music was over, I asked her for another dance. She said yes again. We danced that one and then another. And another. Somewhere in the fifth dance she told me her name was Casey. *(Her birth name was Helen, but she preferred Casey, and so did I.)* A few dances later when "In the Blue of the Evening" wound down, I asked if I could show her the way home. She smiled broadly and said I could. Then she added, "I'm here with a friend, but I'm sure she'd be happy to stay with me tonight."

Her girlfriend had a car, so I drove to the girl's apartment where her mother lived and we all talked for the rest of the evening. Then I asked Casey, "How about lunch tomorrow, or dinner, or something? I'm only going to be here a little bit longer." I didn't know how I could pull it off, but I knew I'd think of some reason to stay one more day. She said okay.

When I got back to the hotel, I had a conversation with my crew chief.

"Al, didn't we have a little problem with number three engine comin' in?" I asked.

"Why, yes, Mike," he intoned, "in fact we did." It turned out he'd met a very nice girl too. "I think we'll need to do a little work on that tomorrow," he added.

"Okay," I said, "we're here another day, then?"

"I'm afraid so," he answered.

When I picked up Casey the following day, she looked even better than the night before. We went to lunch in a nice downtown cafeteria, where I found out she was just as much of a talker as I was. She was also a good dresser and had a spectacular figure. Her brunette hair shimmered from the light through the window. Her laughter was infectious. We spent more time talking than eating.

I got back to the hotel late that night, and the following day we managed to get the engine fixed and off we went to Harrisburg. I'm not sure if it was a run of bad luck or a lapse in production quality control at Boeing, but on our return trip from Harrisburg our brand new B-17 developed a nasty engine vibration. It just didn't feel right, so we decided it was best to make a maintenance stop in Kansas City again, … just in case. After landing, my crew chief and I got out and looked over the plane.

"We really need to check this out," said Al, "to be sure it's all right when we get back to Yuma."

"Yeah," I replied, "better safe than sorry."

The problem turned out to be more serious than we thought, and we had to stay in Kansas City two more days. Casey and I toured around Kansas City mostly on foot. We dodged streetcars, roamed the isles of Lerner department store, explored the old Hay Market, and strolled through Fairmont Park … all very interesting to me since I came from a country town. We mostly walked and talked and then talked some more. After a hamburger and malt in a Main Street café, we caught an early movie at the Foly Theater. I didn't pay much attention to the movie and can't remember the name of it.

I told Casey about my family, and she told me about hers. Her dad was retired, and her mother never worked outside of the home. *(But boy could she cook!)* They were both offspring of German immigrants two generations removed. They came from a small town in Austria when it was the Astro-Hungarian Empire. When the Habsburgs took over, they forced the German farmers to confess their loyalty to the new rulers, or else. They decided on the "or else" and immigrated to America. Casey grew up in Kansas City and now worked as a secretary for Blue Cross Insurance.

They were not wealthy, but they had a nice house and provided for their five children. They liked me immediately, maybe because I was a fighter pilot, but I couldn't be sure. When they found out I came from a farming area of Pennsylvania, I think that reassured them I would not be trouble. When it was time to leave, I reluctantly said goodbye to Casey. Back in Yuma the next day, I immediately called Casey and told her what a great time I had. She said she did too, and that she'd like to see me again.

• • •

Somewhere in the midst of my life in the army, flight training, Yuma, meeting Casey and her parents, I must have acquired a new perspective of life. Through my many months in the service with some hardship and loneliness, I realized all I had before I left home.

June 18, 1944

Dear Dad,

Today is Father's Day. I've often thought about writing this letter but never quite got around to it. When I was home, enjoying everything that seems so important when you don't have it, I failed to realize just how much you were doing for me. Neither did I recognize the motive behind your discipline, which suddenly becomes so clear when I think about it now. You could have done many things differently, but you couldn't have improved your method of raising a family and preparing them for what you knew they must face in their future.... Remember how we used to get up at four in the morning and walk down the Blue Eye or Mead Run by daybreak, or the hikes we used to take in the fall to get butternuts, hickory nuts, and blackberries? It's these simple things that I miss most. As I got older, and started driving, a new method of keeping me in line was presented (and I needed someone to keep me in line). The most important thing you did for me was to teach me that I must make my own decisions regarding right and wrong It may be irregular, but I hope it isn't anything else for a son to thank his father for his boyhood training and way of life. I'm glad that you are my father.

Your son, Howard

= 4 =

CASEY

After I returned from Kansas City, I constantly stayed in touch with Casey. I also kept up my campaign to be sent overseas, which went on from January 1943 through summer 1944, when I finally got results.

August 2, 1944

Dear Mom and Dad,

Since I called the other night I have been busy packing and getting ready to go someplace. You would no doubt like to know where I'm going – well, that makes three of us. We aren't even given the slightest idea of where we will end up and probably we won't know until we arrive. I'm sending my barracks bag home with things I won't need and won't be allowed to take.

Love, Howard

Now that I was about to ship out, I realized my time in Yuma wasn't a total loss. I'd trained a lot of pilots and checked out in all sorts of planes, such as the A-25 dive bomber, the P-40, P-39, B-26, and the B-17. Such diverse knowledge would help me in the future. Of course, the best part about Yuma was meeting Casey.

My orders stated I would report for final training on the P-47 at Harding Field in Baton Rouge, Louisiana, and then transfer to the European theater. It was a bittersweet moment when I called Casey and told her my news. There I was, talking to the first serious girlfriend I ever had, essentially telling her goodbye because I was going off to war. Since we talked about it a few times already, she didn't get all emotional, and, seriously, I wasn't that broken up since I was finally going to do what I'd trained for over the past three years. I told her I'd get a couple of weeks' vacation before shipping out and wanted to spend half of it with her after seeing my parents. To my delight, she said she'd like that very much.

Casey, 1942

A week before my vacation, however, the army notified all pilots bound for Europe that their leaves had been canceled and to report for duty immediately. We knew the reason soon enough when we gathered around the radio to hear President Roosevelt announce the immense Allied invasion of a fifty-mile stretch of the Normandy coast. He said as much as he could, but stopped short of revealing the numbers. Later it would be known as "D-Day," when one-hundred-seventy-five thousand men with a fleet of five thousand ships and landing craft, fifty thousand vehicles, and eleven thousand planes, took part in the invasion. It would be one of the largest efforts of its type in history, resulting from an uncommon level of cooperation among several nations. When Roosevelt finished, we knew we were closer to achieving our common goal of defeating Nazi Germany, and now I would be part of it.

Casey took the news well enough, and to my further delight, said she'd like to visit me at the transition school in Baton Rouge. I agreed, of course, and a few days later she took an overnight train that arrived at 6 a.m. She'd sent a telegram before she left indicating her arrival time, but no one in headquarters told me. I didn't know she was there until I got a call telling me a young lady was in the office and wanted to see me.

She stayed in the bachelor officer's quarters, and we ate at the officers' club, which she thought was first rate. *(So did I.)* We occasionally talked about marriage but realized it was not something we could finalize at the time. I told her I had feelings for her but said it was not right to promise marriage to a woman right before heading to war. As sacrificial and romantic as it might have sounded to her, that's how I really felt.

"Look," I said, "we don't know if I'm coming back or not, do we? In fact, chances are pretty good I might not. So why should you be married to a guy that just got killed in Germany. That doesn't make sense."

I knew guys who did just that. They said to their girlfriends, "Oh, this could be my last trip, and maybe I'll never see you again. Let's get married." On that basis they could sleep with them for a while. Well, to me that was both wrong and corny, but a lot of guys did it. Instead, Casey and I agreed to write to each other often. Although

I didn't specifically ask her to marry me, we kind of knew we were heading in that direction. I said if I got back all right, that marriage might happen.

I'm glad we did what we did, because you can learn a lot about people when you write letters. You can talk all day and do lots of things together, but when you write your thoughts down, you say things in ways you wouldn't say in conversation. A lot more thought goes into communication before it becomes an indelible, written word. You describe situations more thoroughly and explain thoughts more deeply. Things that might sound corny in conversation can come across quite well in a letter.

While Casey and I had established a degree of trust and promised to write each other on a regular basis, one important matter remained unresolved: how could I tell my parents she was Catholic?

Our four days flew by, and all too soon I had to report to New York to catch a troop ship to the United Kingdom. At the end of our last evening, I took her to the train station, where we hugged a very long time. As I said, I'd never had a steady girlfriend until Casey, so when she came into my life, I was altogether smitten and surprised. The feeling was wonderful when we were together and painful when we said goodbye. That gal really got through to me.

≡ 5 ≡

TROOP CARRIER

Since all the planes were engaged in the war effort, there was nothing available to fly us to England. Instead, I was sent to New York where I boarded a ship named the *Cristobal*, a 493-foot, 10,100-ton converted cargo ship that held the seventeen hundred of us bound for Europe. *(After the war, the Cristobal would be modified to carry 119 war brides and 101 dependent children from Europe to the United States.)*

As an officer, I was accustomed to having my own room, or at least a nice one that I shared with another officer. When I boarded the *Cristobal* and inquired about my quarters, the quartermaster told us they had a special room reserved for us. "That's very nice," I thought. I followed the directions down several decks and through a long corridor to my "special" room, occupied by eight other officers. The cabin was at most twelve-by-twelve feet, and our hammocks were stacked three-high against the walls. We also shared a community bathroom, called a *head* by the navy.

The ship was crowded and hot. It also smelled from the vomit of the vast number of men who got seasick. Seldom did I walk from one place to another without being assaulted by the stench of vomit. I believe my time in the air with the pitch and yaw of an airplane conditioned me for the rolling sea, so the only time I felt queasy was when I saw the contents of someone's stomach all over the deck.

At least I could walk topside at specified hours for some fresh air, although they restricted the number of men and the duration at any one time.

The food wasn't first class, but it was adequate, since I was a farm boy accustomed to eating most anything. I pitied the highbrows from New York City with all those fancy restaurants. In fact, I'd never been in a *real* restaurant, certainly not in Youngsville, so I couldn't compare. My best reference was, I suppose, the cafeteria where I took Casey in Kansas City.

On board there was a lot of time to read. A few magazines and books were available in a small library, but we mostly traded books with others. We did get to hear some great music, though. There were several really good musicians among the seventeen hundred of us who didn't mind playing a few tunes. There was an old piano in the chow hall, and they'd play whatever they knew, often by request. They banged out Artie Shaw, Tommy Dorsey, Glen Miller, Bing Crosby, and even Stan Kenton's "Shoo Shoo Baby." When a player's fingers got tired, another guy jumped on the bench and picked up where the other left off. It became one big sing-along fest, helping us to briefly forget about lovers back home, the discomforts of the ship, and the war. If I closed my eyes, the smell of cigarette smoke and the loud singing took me back to former times with friends. After several hours of our shipboard cabaret, I crawled into my swaying hammock and slept quite well.

Throughout the trip, I made quick visits to the head, took fast showers, and skipped shaving entirely. As cramped as we felt, neither I nor any of my cabin mates complained about our living conditions, especially since the rest of the soldiers on board had it far worse, having been crammed like sardines in tiny, ill-ventilated cabins. After all, we were on our way to fight a war, and no one was deemed better than anyone else.

Finally, after staring at miles of ocean for days on end, we reached the coast of Scotland, our destination. I enjoyed watching the land drift by as we cruised fifty miles up the River Clyde to Glasgow. We disembarked at the commercial docks of the city, climbed on a train (with comfortable seats), and rattled down to New Castle in northern England. It was mid-August, and the English countryside looked green and beautiful.

Settled into slightly more comfortable quarters, I spent the next month on my final checkout for the P-47. I also took some operational training from a pilot who flew in combat. Eventually I was assigned to a squadron on the continent; most likely it would be in recently liberated France. Up until then, most fighter pilots were flown to their respective bases, but with all the recent paratrooper drops, towed gliders, and supply transports, there were no flights available to get me to my base. Once again, I would travel by boat.

OMAHA BEACH

After an all-day train trip from Newcastle to Southampton, a group of fighter pilots, bomber pilots, transport jockeys—about 250 of us in all—boarded a Landing Ship Tank (LST) for France. The ride was actually very good, mostly because the navy treated us so well. The navy fed us well too …, better than anything I had in the army. Several hours and 120 miles later, the LST bumped against the shore of Omaha Beach and continued to claw its way up to dry land. When the front end flopped down on the sand, we just walked off, not even wetting the soles of our shoes. It was quite a contrast to the unbelievable chaos of D-Day two months earlier. We walked up the beach and gathered to wait beneath a camouflaged awning. Eventually an army lieutenant colonel walked up and, without fanfare, shouted,

"I don't know what the arrangements will be," he pointed his thumb toward the southeast, "but Paris is in that direction. I want all of you to be there within one week. I don't know how you'll get there, but it's up to you. Hitchhike for all I care." Two of his aides started handing out pieces of paper. "I'll see you all at this address," he said. "Remember, one week." The address was a school in the middle of Paris, although I can't recall the name.

Not far from where we landed was a small airbase in a town named Picauville, the first town liberated by the Allied forces during the Normandy invasion. The Army Corps built an advanced landing area there as soon as it was cleared, and the base was first used by the 405th Fighter Group with P-47 Thunderbolts. This was the plane I would eventually fly over Germany. The original plan was to catch a flight from Picauville to Paris for orientation, but Picauville didn't have any transport planes either, which is why the colonel told us to take a hike.

Age 23, 1944

≡ 6 ≡

THUMBING TO PARIS

Bob Fredette and Burt Sadowski were two friends I trained with back in the states. Quite by chance, we wound up on the same landing craft from England, so the three of us decided we would hitchhike to Paris. Like all Americans in that area, we had all heard a lot about Paris: the wine, the Eiffel Tower, and the Moulin Rouge. So it was kind of exciting. One of the guys on the ship—an American who spoke French—told us Moulin Rouge meant "red windmill," which didn't make sense until we saw it.

Our first step was to hike over the sand dunes to the top of the broad beach and trek through some farmland until we came to a dirt road. We walked a few miles further until we came to a paved highway. Sure enough, we came across numerous army supply trucks speeding back and forth. Since we didn't intend to walk all the way to Paris—24 miles, the same distance as between Southampton and Omaha Beach—we stuck out our thumbs. Soon, a six-by-six cargo truck stopped to pick us up.

"Where you heading?" asked the African American behind the wheel. We told him.

"Okay, climb in the back, there should be plenty of room."

When the three of us piled in the rear of the truck, there was barely enough room to squat on the floor between all the boxes of supplies. About half way to Paris the guy called to us through the rear window.

"I have to turn off now. The unit I'm delivering is here. Good luck."

We quickly got another ride with another African-American. It turned out most of the drivers were black, and they were all great guys. One of them told us we were on the route they called the "Red Ball Express"—the road for hauling supplies from the beaches to units in France and beyond. I noticed the trucks sported logos with red balls here and there, and the route we followed was punctuated by signs along the way with the same red balls. Apparently the road was closed to all other traffic except Allied forces. That made sense because in the Allied race across France to get Hitler, resupply of ammunition, fuel, and food had to be fast and steady.

We arrived in Paris late that afternoon, tired and hungry. The last driver didn't know where the school was, so he wished us good luck and left us somewhere in the center of the city. There were no taxis around, and none of us spoke French, but we knew enough to get by with the help of a little booklet they gave us before we landed in France. We finally managed to get directions, and, sure enough, we found the schoolhouse tucked away in a back street not far from the famous Champs-Elysées. The same lieutenant colonel we met at the beach was already there, and he was just as cordial.

"You can go anywhere you want as long as you get your asses back here by eight in the morning."

That gave us a lot of leeway really, so we thought we'd try out Paris on our first night. The one question on our minds was, "Where is the Moulin Rouge?" We asked around, and one kind old man pointed down the street and said it was only a few blocks away. As we walked the streets and boulevards of the city, we took in all the amazing architecture of Paris. It was surprising how well preserved the city looked after four brutal years of Hitler. When the French resistance was about to liberate Paris (with a little help from our Fourth Infantry

Division), Hitler ordered the city defended to the last man, swearing the city would never fall into Allied hands. "If it does," he shouted, "there should be nothing left but a field of ruins."

When the fall was imminent, the Nazi general in charge began laying explosives under bridges and landmarks in accordance with Hitler's orders, but he refused to detonate them. It was rumored he didn't want to be known in history as the man who destroyed Europe's most celebrated city. Instead, the general—named Choltitz—signed a formal surrender not long before the Allies arrived. As green as I was to all things French, I couldn't help but appreciate that German general for saving Paris. It was the most beautiful city I'd ever seen.

THE RED WINDMILL

We turned a corner and suddenly there it was … right on *#82 Boulevard de Clichy.* It was a red, cartoon-like building with four big windmill blades drooping over the sidewalk, except the blades weren't spinning. I wasn't sure they were supposed to, or maybe the Germans switched off the motor. We went in, sat down at a table not far from the stage, and ordered French champagne for the first time in our lives. The smiling, tuxedoed waiter delivered it at once. We poured three glasses, toasted, and drank. Then the next bottle arrived, and we drank that. Half way through the third bottle, we wondered when something would happen on the stage. Sometime during our fourth bottle, a small orchestra in the balcony struck up a rousing tune, as a huge trap door on the stage dropped down. Next, a platform started to emerge with a big, beautiful white horse standing on it. Seated on its back was an equally beautiful creature: a smiling, waving, very naked, blonde-haired woman. The crowd went wild. I turned to my buddy and said, "I like this place. Let's have another bottle!"

A male guide dressed in leotards led the horse in circles around the stage while the woman kept waving and smiling. They made three rounds until Godiva and her steed disappeared behind the curtains. As soon as they were gone, about fifteen topless women pranced around the stage and danced cabaret style to the deafening whoops and cheers from the audience. The more champagne we consumed, the better the show. That went on for another hour or so until we realized how bombed we were and thought it best to get back to the schoolhouse while we still could. Somehow our collective memories guided us back to the right address, because I woke up in my bunk at the right place. We all made the eight o'clock muster, heads pounding.

We spent the next four nights in Paris engaged in more sober endeavors. We explored the shops of the city and tried out various restaurants. I discovered the French really did know how to cook, just like I had always heard. In fact most of their food was better than anything I ever had before, hands down. They knew how to take very little and make a lot out of it.

• • •

Between the time we landed at Omaha Beach and our stay at the school in Paris, the 405th Fighter Group relocated from its original location in Picauville to Saint-Dizier, France. Saint-Dizier stood about 180 miles east of Paris, oddly enough in the middle of the champagne district of France. Seems our training at the Moulin Rouge and other night spots was good for something after all. Four days after we arrived in Paris, a transport vehicle took me and the other members designated for the 405th to our new home in Saint-Dizier. Our carefree days in the City of Lights would be the last for a very long time. For me, the war had finally begun.

Part III

★ ★ ★

ABOVE THE THIRD REICH

July, 1944 – October 15, 1945

☰ 1 ☰

PLENTY OF HOURS

The Nazis first captured Saint-Dizier and its adjoining airfield from the French during the Battle of France in 1940. They went on to convert it to a Luftwaffe base and expanded it significantly during their occupation. Although liberated only weeks before our arrival, the town of Saint-Dizier was actually well preserved. Damage to the airfield was minimal too. Since our forces were in such a hurry to move toward Berlin, the retreating Germans didn't have time to destroy it. Later, prior to D-Day, American planes bombed and strafed the Saint-Dizier airfield with B-26 Marauders, medium-sized bombers, and P-47 Thunderbolts. The reason the Americans did this was that their heavy B-17 and B-24 bombers flying out of English bases passed within interception range of the Luftwaffe aircraft based at Saint-Dizier. They timed the airfield attacks for maximum effect to keep their interceptors on the ground to give relatively free air space for our heavy bombers.

Allied forces seized the town and the airfield on September 14, 1944, and soon the Ninth Engineer Command repaired the runways and facilities. When they finished, the field was designated Advanced Landing Ground A-64. Although the 405th already flew missions out of the field, it was formally turned over to the Ninth Air Force on October 9. When I arrived, I found thirty-foot wide concrete runways with an adequate length of eight thousand feet. It could handle almost anything taking off or landing. It seems the Germans did a good job of preparing the base for our timely arrival.

After I settled in and got to know some of the other pilots, I found I had a lot more experience than the average P-47 flyer. Although I detested hanging around Yuma for all those months, I realized I'd racked up a lot of hours by flying all sorts of planes in the training program. With my experience on P39s, P38s, P40s, and the P-47, I knew a thing or two about aircraft. By the time I entered combat, I had eighteen hundred hours under my belt. On the other hand, pilots fresh out of training arrived in Saint-Dizier with five hundred hours, maximum. With my hours, I could try a lot of things in the cockpit that other guys might not be trained to do.

We operated out of that base for the next six months, which was a relatively long period of time for that kind of assignment. The speed with which General Patton's army moved across France would normally cause us to relocate much sooner. Patton seemed to have bogged down in a place called Metz, not far from us. Apparently, the city was well fortified, and Patton was having a hard time getting through. The more time he spent on taking the city, the more time the Germans would have to regroup further east. I would soon have the opportunity to see Metz at very close range.

THE JUG

The 405th had three squadrons of twenty-five P-47's, for a total of seventy-five planes. During most missions, we ran three or four flights of four ships each. *(We often referred to planes as ships.)* In every case, the flights consisted of the powerful P-47 Thunderbolt fighter plane ... a machine I would come to appreciate more and more as the war progressed.

But before I continue, I think this magnificent plane deserves some back story. By the time I arrived in France in 1944, the Thunderbolt had improved significantly since the start of the war. It was a heavy, almost overpowered warbird that packed a devastating punch. With its Pratt & Whitney R-2800 eighteen-cylinder radial engine, it could handle most anything in terms of payload and speed combined. From my own experience, which I'll discuss later, the Thunderbolt was capable of taking a terrible beating while remaining in the air. Although it didn't feel like it at times, the cockpit was roomier than most comparable fighters. Some pilots even considered it comfortable— freezing air temperatures aside. Although heavier than comparable fighters, its speed topped nearly 425 mph. Our Thunderbolts were also fitted with water injection cooling, which added several hundred horsepower for emergency use. Lastly, the bubble canopy they added before I arrived in France allowed for greater visibility front to back. Until the engineers made that change, many pilots bitterly complained about the lack of visibility between four o'clock and eight o'clock, a 130-degree blind spot that sometimes proved fatal.

The Thunderbolt's typical bomb load was one five-hundred-pound bomb under each wing, but for special missions it could carry one thousand-pound bomb under each wing. We also carried eight fifty-caliber machine guns—four on each wing—with four hundred rounds per gun. That's a lot of potential destruction. Occasionally we carried 110-gallon auxiliary fuel tanks, adding another eight hundred pounds. So with one thousand pounds of bombs, eight fully loaded machine guns, and possibly more fuel, there was substantial weight. Fortunately the plane's R-2800 engine could handle it all and still be light on its feet.

There was yet another advantage to the plane bestowed upon it by its design engineers—a half-inch thick piece of aluminum called a *spoiler*. The spoiler was, in essence, an emergency brake designed to pull the P-47 out of an uncontrolled, high-speed dive. Thirty inches long and four inches wide, the strip was located on the underside of the wing not far from the fuselage, and attached by more hinges than you could count. Here's how it worked: when a P-47 found itself in what we called a *compressibility dive*, the pilot lost all control of the plane: ailerons, rudder, flaps, etc. Everything ceased to function as the plane raced toward the Earth. That usually happened when the plane reached or exceeded its *red line*, a maximum speed of around five hundred miles per hour. The only way to avoid a crash was to push a special button tucked beneath the throttle module on the left side of the cockpit.

I used the spoiler for the first time in northern England during the transition time after I arrived from the States. As a replacement pilot, I had to be checked out again on the P-47 by experienced pilots who had flown in combat. When they covered the part about the spoiler, I became fascinated. How could a thin strip of metal save an entire plane going five hundred mph straight down?

I answered my question shortly after completing the course. I went up to twenty-five thousand feet—plenty of altitude in case something went wrong—and intentionally put the plane into a steep dive. As the engine whined with higher and higher velocity, I watched the airspeed indicator swing from the left side of the dial to the right. Sure enough, when I approached red line, my controls stopped functioning. They just froze up. As the air traveled over and under the surfaces at such a speed, any attempt to regain control was lost. I have to say it was a very disconcerting feeling. "Did they really test this thing?" I wondered. It was too late to ask such questions because I'd reached the point of no return. The spoiler *had* to work. I can't say I was afraid exactly, but my emotions were best described as "deeply concerned." When I had enough, I pushed the button.

I heard a powerful *Bzzzzzzt!* from below, as the electric ramrod shoved the spoiler from its pocket. Like the broad flaps that slow an airline on approach, the two slices of extended metal immediately began to disrupt air flow. The plane trembled slightly, as disturbed airflow hit the horizontal and vertical stabilizers, allowing them to bite the air once again. The stick responded in kind, and I regained control. I pulled back and gradually levelled out at eight thousand feet, completely out of the dive and flying level with room to spare.

Some might say that was a crazy thing to do, but by then I'd become a constant student of flying and I worked hard at learning as much as I could. Part of my self-imposed training had me push the envelope with things like the spoiler, so testing its limits wasn't risky in my estimation. Obviously, it had been placed there long before, and some pilots lived to tell how well it worked. So I wouldn't call it daring; I'd call it a calculated risk. It was not that different from testing an escape chute from an airliner or dropping a lifeboat from a ship. If I ever really needed it, I knew it would work.

As the war continued, and the Thunderbolt gained more fame, the fighter came to be known as "The Jug."—first by the Brits who said the fat fuselage reminded them of a milk jug, and later by adoring US Army Air Corps pilots who thought the plane was a veritable juggernaut. Whichever impression was correct, the fact that it earned such a noble nickname testifies to its great value.

Throughout the war, nearly sixteen thousand Thunderbolts were built in three US locations. They were used in every operating theater of the war, serving as bomber escort; close air support; and, in my case, hit-and-run bombing and strafing missions throughout France and Germany. By war's end, the plane's safety record was nothing short of astounding – only about 7 percent of all Thunderbolts were lost in action—but our squadron safety record would be the exception since we always seemed to get the lion's share of the action.

During rare quiet times in the cockpit, I thought about the thousands of hands that put this amazing machine together, working in concert in factories and assembly lines across the nation. There I was, riding that wonderful war horse through enemy skies, often talking to it like I would converse with a faithful friend.

FINALLY DOWN TO BUSINESS

The morning of October 3, 1944, was unusually cold for that time of year in northern France. In fact, it felt more like Youngsville, Pennsylvania, in the dead of winter—chilling to the bone. I shouldn't have been surprised, though, since France occupied the same latitude as Newfoundland. At least the mess tent was heated, and my 7:30 a.m. breakfast was more than decent. They served pancakes, ham, scrambled eggs, and toast. I wasn't very big on oatmeal or cream of wheat, and though we were in France, quiche would never be part of my diet.

It had been almost two weeks since I arrived in Saint-Dizier, and I was about to be briefed on our mission that day—my first mission. As I approached the tent, I wondered, "If it's this cold on the ground, how bad will it be in an unheated cockpit of a P-47?" At altitude, I'd probably feel the outside temperature through the metal skin of the plane, as if I were naked. I hoped our standard issue flight clothing would do the job, since I was relatively slight in stature compared to the average male. As I wrote to my parents:

October 3, 1944

Dear Mom and Dad,
  It's so cold at night that I have trouble keeping warm with four blankets. My helmet, which I use as a wash basin, had ice in the bottom of it this morning.

Love, Howard

I never thought I'd complain about the cold after those endless months in Yuma, suffering in temperatures above 100°F.

Preflight briefing told us that we would work with a ground operation they called "Gasket." Various units we worked with went by code names for obvious reasons. Some of them were hilarious. Gasket was an outfit northeast of the town of Nancy, about eighty-five miles due east of our base. We'd fly to their location and find out what they wanted us to bomb and strafe. I was to fly in Red, meaning our flight with four planes would be closest to the ground. White and Blue flights would be above us. Lieutenants Greene and Thomas were my wingmen.

When we arrived around 11:15 a.m., our communication with Gasket was cut off, so we took our instructions from "Pailful," the code name of another outfit nearby. They directed us to a heavily wooded area dubbed U-7855 on our flight maps. The Germans were forming there in preparation for a counterattack, so we proceeded to thoroughly bomb and strafe the area. After we dropped all our bombs—twenty-four in total—and we were about to return to base, we observed a huge yellow and red ball, some sort of explosion. Later we surmised it was a fuel depot. One of the planes piloted by Lieutenant Fredette flew too close to the explosion and received damage from the bomb fragments. He got back to the base unharmed, however.

The next three days dogged us with cold, rain, and fog, typical weather for that part of France at that time of the year.

October 5, 1944

Dear Mom and Dad,

France is one large mud hole. Just as it starts to dry up, the rain comes again. Since I've been here, it's averaged at least one rainstorm per day. My sympathy for the doughboys in their foxholes is greater now than it has ever been.

Love, Howard

The skies were clear on October 7, so the 405th made the best of it by flying five missions that day. I flew Blue on my first mission,

meaning I was on the top of the formation. The "Ironclad" outfit
directed us to a target two miles away to a hill outside of Jeandelincourt,
just north of Nancy, where enemy installations and guns were ripping
our troops. Red and White flights bombed and strafed the installation
and went on to hit railroad cars. One White had trouble releasing
his bombs, and, after several attempts, managed to let them go.
Meanwhile my Blue flight had the "top cover" position, so we dodged
all the flak thrown our way from the installation. The Germans were
fairly accurate, and flak shells exploded all around us, but no one got
hit badly. The leader of Red did get two flak holes but was able to get
back to base safely.

Right after lunch on the same day, my flight scrambled back to
the town of Nancy to locate and bomb enemy artillery, but when we
arrived at the approximate location, there was nothing to be found.
This meant the artillery was mobile, or camouflaged by thick forest.
Since we were out that far, we proceeded to the area of Metz where
Patton still battled the nearly impregnable forts. As soon as we arrived,
we were met by heavy flak, but we couldn't find enemy artillery.

Back in the area of Metz the following day, we observed several
of our B-26 bombers pummeling the forts. The continuing assault on
that city proved to be a real sticking point for Patton's advance, and
soon the 405th would be directly involved in it.

═ 2 ═

THE SHACK

Living and sleeping during the legendary northern European winter of 1944–45, when the Battle of the Bulge would take place, was almost unbearable. Saint-Dizier was 120 miles northeast of that battle site, so our bitter cold started even earlier, in September. Our fighter squadron consisted of about 250 men, including mechanics, pilots, armorers, and administrators. We all lived in tents with heaters that supposedly put out heat, but it was never enough. We slept on cots, which I quickly discovered were the worst things to sleep on in cold weather. There is no insulation between the bottom of the canvas and the floor, so although I had several blankets over me, freezing air had almost direct contact with my backside.

By early November it got worse, so I decided to make a few improvements. I didn't ask permission from anyone but instead asked my buddy, Bob Fredette, to help me build a place to sleep in. He agreed, since anything was better than a tent. Over the next few weeks, we scavenged leftover wood from a French warehouse near the airfield and started hammering boards together. When the frame was complete, we found some tarpaper and secured several layers over the roof beams. Then we needed a door, but instead of a regular walk-through, we built a trap door—the kind dogs use to get in the house, only bigger. When we finished building it, we had a handsome, six-by-six foot shack, about triple the size of your standard outhouse and just big enough to squeeze in two cots.

We also needed heat. Fortunately, some of the old buildings left by the Germans still had heaters. We requisitioned one of them, hauled it to our shack, cut a hole in the roof, and installed the chimney. It was a tight fit, and we had to be careful not to set the place on fire or burn our feet. In the end it worked beautifully, and we finally slept through the night without freezing our butts off. I could even take a shower with hot water from the stove. Using my steel helmet, I stood on the floor and poured steaming hot water over my head. Then I lathered, rinsed, and repeated. The whole experience was sublime, and I felt like a king.

So there we were: tents lined up in military dress-right-dress across the field, with a rickety shack on the end looking like something out of Appalachia. I guess that was one of the upsides of being a pilot: we enjoyed relative freedom to make our own sleeping situation better if we didn't break any rules. As long as we showed up on time for preflight briefings, we were pretty much left to our own devices.

My Shack, St Dizier (far left)

Unfortunately, right before we moved into our shack, Bob Fredette was shot down on his third mission. I found out later he was captured and made a POW, but, as far as I knew, he was still alive. No one else wanted to fill his spot in my shack, so now I had it all to myself.

• • •

There was no such thing as an officer's club, so to satisfy our need to talk or pass the bottle, we sat around on boxes in the corner of a supply tent to chew the fat. So there we were, officers and gentlemen, fighter pilots and heroes—huddled around cases of canned tuna or tomato paste, bragging about our amazing deeds. It was all we had to keep our spirits up, and when we weren't flying missions, sleeping, eating, or trying to stay clean, we gathered in that tent and talked. In a sense, I suppose I was one of the leaders. One day after I finished a particularly long story (probably an account of a hunting escapade in the forest), Frank Steinburg turned to me and said, "You know what Spencer, if bullshit was snow, you'd be a blizzard." I often looked around the room at the other men and knew they were just about the best bunch of pilots anyone could find anywhere.

While we had the luxury of good, warm food and I had my own little heated shack, the guys holding out in the fierce battle in the Ardennes brought a whole new definition to cold. In warm weather, the Ardennes—a mountain range with vast forests in northeastern France, Belgium, Luxembourg, and Germany—was a real vacation destination. But in that winter of 1944-45, it was treacherous. Snow, ice, and subfreezing weather set the scene for one of the most desperate battles ever fought by American troops. It must have been like Valley Forge but with a tragic, modern twist. Tank turrets froze and men had to chip them free of ice. Frozen breach blocks on rifles wouldn't move up and down. M-1 rifles didn't work until soldiers pounded their bolts back and forth with the hard casing of a grenade. When escape hatches and tank doors stuck fast, soldiers used blow torches to thaw them out. Ice formed in gas tanks and clogged fuel lines. Countless soldiers suffered frostbitten feet. By comparison, we of the 405th lived in palaces.

• • •

Casey and I continued to write to each other, and in the midst of the cold it was wonderful to receive her letters filled with warm care and concern. She asked many questions, as if wanting to know exactly what I was going through. I told her as much as I could without compromising any military secrets. As we continued to write, I became aware of the need to be transparent with my parents. They knew very little about this woman who had already taken much of my heart.

November 2, 1944

Hello Dad,

We might call this a man-to-man discussion instead of a son's letter to his father. There is something I have wanted to tell you for a long time. The girl I intend to marry is Catholic, and neither of us wish to change our religion. I don't know your and Mother's feelings in regard to this because it was never discussed. It's probably no secret to you that I have wanted to get married since I graduated from high school, but until now I was not only unprepared for the responsibilities, but I hadn't found the girl I was ready to live with every day for fifty-plus years of married life. I think I have observed the field successfully in the last five years and know what I want. Casey is that girl. She doesn't drink or smoke, and she has the highest ideals of any girl I have ever known. Most important of all, I think she wants to marry me.

Love, Howard

A BLIND WINGMAN

By mid-November our missions took us further afield, and our targets became more interesting, if I could put it that way. Here's what Major Abraham wrote in his debriefing on November 19. It was one to remember:

```
Contacted "Flabby," who gave us "Zebra"
to work with. Zebra's radio was weak so
"Liver'" gave us the message to bomb
at Q-2743. "Bygone" was circling this
town and advised against bombing there
but gave us Q-3043 and Q-3141 to bomb
instead. Because enemy installations
were sighted in both Francaltroff and
Erstroff, Red flight hit the town of
Francaltroff with seven five-hundred-
pound bombs, while White flight hit
Erstroff with napalm and fragment
bombs. Erstroff was a burning inferno
after the bombing, as White flight had
all direct hits. White flight strafed
and destroyed two military tanks near
St. Avolo. White two was hit by flak
and bailed out safely near Toul after
his plane caught fire.
```

I have to say that White flight's direct hits, which were my doing, and were the result, in a large part, to all my hours of flight training in Yuma. I guess I had learned the fine art of hitting the target.

• • •

On November 25 we flew about an hour and a half up to the west side of the Rhine River. During the preflight briefing, we were told our mission was to be an armed reconnaissance in the Frankfurt area. On approach, however, the cloud cover thickened, and we had to go above it, so we bombed small marshalling yards in the southeast of the city. We also strafed trains and various vehicles in the area; in effect, we aimed at anything that looked remotely like it could have a military function.

Red two, piloted by Lieutenant Sides, got a little too close to the bomb blasts, and some of the bomb fragments hit the plane's oil line. I was fairly close and watched the spewing oil completely douse its canopy. I knew Lieutenant Sides couldn't see, and when his plane began to wobble, I flew closer and radioed him.

"You all right?"

"Hell no. I can't see."

"Nothing at all?" I knew that but had to hear it anyway.

"Nothing, just the instruments, but not much. I have blood in my eyes too."

"Listen," I said, "I'll come close, and we'll fly section back to the base. Keep an eye on your instruments, and I'll escort you."

I moved in closer until my right wing was about eight feet from his and slightly in front. It looked like he could keep his plane steady enough. Formation flying was one of the first things we learned after we became familiar with our aircraft. World War I pilots started flying in formation when they escorted reconnaissance aircraft over enemy territory. They found that sticking close together reduced casualties. Eventually they learned flying in pairs—called *section*—reduced losses and increased victories.

"Can you see me, at least a little?" I asked.

"Yeah, I can barely see the tip of your wing. I'm on instruments, sort of."

P-47 instruments were basic and not very reliable.

"Good," I replied, "we've got about twenty minutes to the base. I'll take you all the way in."

My only concern was that German fighter pilots would find us; it was easy to spot somebody in trouble. At eighteen thousand feet, we'd be slow moving targets.

"We're going in lower," I radioed, "decline with me at ten degrees."

"Roger," he replied.

I slowly pressed the stick forward. He followed, keeping more or less the same distance wing-to-wing. When we reached two thousand feet, I levelled off.

"How you doing?" I asked.

"You're really blurry, but I still see you." His voice was calm.

"Okay, now I'm making a ninety-degree right turn. Stay close."

I made the slow turn and straightened out so the base was straight ahead. There was no activity from the ground or air and soon we'd be out of enemy territory. I looked over my shoulder and Sides was right there.

"We're about twenty minutes out," I said. "I'm gonna take you straight onto the tarmac."

"Okay, Mike. I'm all for that."

"I'll tell you when to drop your flaps and your wheels. You just keep position, and I'll watch what you're doing."

Lieutenant Sides was now my wingman, and I was the leader. He had to follow every move I made, although it would be next to impossible with no outside visibility and blood clouding his eyes. It was also risky. With only six feet between wings, if he made a quick, wrong move, it could be over for both of us. After all the hours of discipline and rule-following, formation flying had to pay off. I radioed Sides every couple of minutes to be sure he was okay and looked back to confirm he remained in the slot. Fortunately, weather was on our side. I spotted the base four miles ahead and radioed Sides.

"Get ready to head for *terra firma*."

"Okay, he said, "I can barely see you."

"Fly with me and don't worry about yourself."

At 120 mph, it only took a couple of minutes until we were on approach. "Going down," I said, and slowly eased the stick forward. "Get ready ... okay, wheels and flaps down! I'll tell you when to cut your power."

The tarmac rose quickly as we descended. I glanced across to Sides and could barely see his fuzzy image leaning forward, concentrating.

"Cut your power," I shouted. I watched his plane nose upward with the decrease of power.

"Pull up a little, and keep your tail down," I instructed. He knew all that of course, but reminding him was all right under the circumstances. He followed my instructions perfectly. When he was about to touch down, I pulled a combat spread to give some distance. After peeling away, I turned to watch him land safely and roll to a halt.

· · ·

The ground crew reached Lieutenant Sides's plane as he attempted to climb from the cockpit. They extracted him the rest of the way and took him to the field hospital, where they cleaned the lacerations around his face and on the exposed parts of his arms. Sides's bandages looked worse than the actual wounds. Since our heads keep large amounts of blood at any given time, a head wound tends to bleed like a gushing hydrant, which explained why he couldn't see. In the end, his injuries weren't serious enough to send him home. The blast not only broke his plane's oil line, it shattered part of the plane's canopy on the opposite side, which I couldn't see.

Apparently someone interviewed Lieutenant Sides, and he told them everything that happened. Later, our group commander called me into his office and told me I would receive the Distinguished Flying

Cross for helping Sides land safely. Well, that was just fine with me, although I was quite happy just being alive and able to fly. After all, that was my job: get up there, drop a couple of bombs, and squeeze off a few hundred rounds with my fifty-calibers if I could. That's what I did, and that's what the other pilots did. It never occurred to me that helping a fellow pilot through a hard time would earn me a medal. I already had a couple of medals anyway, awarded each time I flew five missions. Eventually I would earn thirteen of them for my eighty-nine total missions. But the Distinguished Flying Cross? I was honored to receive it of course, even if it seemed a bit over the top. Three days after the incident, I managed to get a few badly needed days off and went to Paris.

November 29, 1944

Dear Mom and Dad,

    Monday I returned from Paris. Periodically a member of a combat crew is allowed a forty-eight-hour pass to Paris. We start out at 7:30 a.m. and ride for several hours in the back of a two and one-half ton truck. I can't remember a colder ride, but once we arrive the ride is soon forgotten. The army has taken over several of the larger hotels and in this way provides rooms and meals. Three officers (pilots) from our squadron went in this time. We had a room to ourselves with three single beds (mattresses, yes, mattresses — the first since I left the United States), and a bathtub in which I would soak for a half hour each time. I took plenty of baths in two days. Downstairs was a dining room with French waiters. It was a wonderful two days just looking around, seeing the sights, and going to some of the better night clubs. We tried to go to the opera, but couldn't get in.

Love, Howard

≡ 3 ≡

NEARLY IMPENETRABLE

General Patton was in a tight spot. With its heavy fortifications and strategic location, the city of Metz became an important point of resistance for the Germans. They mounted a strong defense to contain the advancing US Third Army while buying time for an organized withdrawal to the Saar region. The battle dragged on, and the German resistance resulted in heavy casualties for both sides.

Metz is situated at the junction of the Moselle and Seille rivers. It has a rich, three- thousand-year history as a military outpost and crossroads dating back to the Romans. The problem for the Allies was the forts—which had been built over a century and a half before—had been strengthened for the First World War I and again for the second. The fortifications had six-foot thick walls with ten-foot thick reinforced concrete roofs. They were covered with as much as twenty feet of earth. New casemates punctuated the ancient walls between several observation cupolas. The batteries—and there were many of them—could shoot anything in any direction due to their rotating steel turrets. Underground tunnels connected the bunkhouses with munitions' storage, eating facilities, and other support structures. Trenches, about thirty-feet deep and thirty-feet wide, surrounded the entire complex. A wide barrier of barbed wire entanglements with numerous gun positons guarded the whole arrangement. No matter what Patton's Third Army threw at them, the Germans held their position. And as long as the Metz forts held, Patton could not advance. That's when our strategists decided to throw a bunch of one-thousand-pound M-65 armor-piercing bombs at them.

Until then, M-65 bombs were carried by heavy bombers to take out dams and railroad bridges. These targets were obtainable from high-altitude planes, but that didn't apply to Metz. To approach that that cauldron of missiles and flak with big, slow, heavy bombers, would be suicide. To accomplish the mission with minimal damage to the Allies would require low, fast, in-and-out strikes. It made sense to the smart guys back in headquarters (who had never flown a mission, by the way) when they decided to load a M-65 bomb under each wing of our P-47s. As dangerous as it would be, it make sense to us.

Metz was about eighty-five miles from Saint-Dizier, and flying there with a normal load of five-hundred-pound bombs and fifty-caliber bullets was still within operational range for a P-47. However, doubling the weight of the bomb load meant we would arrive at target with very little airtime to do anything else. The solution? We would quickly build an airstrip in Luxembourg, not far from Metz. The plan? We would fly P-47s in from Saint-Dizier, refuel at Luxembourg, load the M-65s, and get down to business with spare time to inflict further damage. Like everything else in that war, the plan wasn't fail-safe, but it made sense. Besides, there was no alternative.

The engineers found a relatively flat field, leveled it off as much as possible, and covered it with twelve-foot-by-fifteen-inch wide, pierced-steel sections. The series of interlocking planks formed a makeshift strip sufficient for takeoff and landing, but just barely. The resulting "runway" was short, uneven, not very wide, and somewhat dangerous. Fortunately the P-47's undercarriage was wide, which helped us maintain control while ferrying two seven-foot long M-65 bombs.

It took longer to take off with the extra payload, so we had to be sure we were airborne by the time we reached the end of our forty-five-hundred-foot runway. The only way it could work was to plant both feet on the brakes hard and apply full throttle, holding it for several seconds at top rpm. Like a growling bulldog held by a leash, the plane rumbled and shook until I released the brakes. I felt the pent-up force as the plane lurched forward. All too soon, the forty-five hundred feet raced by, and when I reached the end—ready or not—I pulled up. It worked. Our situation was similar to what Jimmy Doolittle faced when his squadron of B-52 bombers took off from the deck of the *USS Hornet* to blitz Tokyo (Doolittle's famous flight turned the tide for the United States from a defensive to an offensive position early in World War II). They revved their engines all the way up before releasing the brakes, and by the time they reached the end of the carrier they had to be airborne or they would fall into the sea. The planes carried a full load of fuel and bombs but forfeited extra ammunition. Their mission was to inflict maximum psychological damage rather than physical damage on Japan. History shows they made a successful run, although a few crashed after they ran out of fuel.

Fuel wasn't our problem, the bomb load was. The P-47 was already heavy, so the extra one thousand pounds of munitions required a tremendous amount of extra power. On the first armed test run, one of our guys didn't make it. Either he didn't reach maximum rpm before releasing the brakes, or he let off on the brakes too early. Whatever the cause, he failed to get airborne and crashed at the end of the runway. Fortunately there was an open field at the end, so he survived. The bombs didn't arm themselves until they were released from the plane, so there was no danger of explosion.

• • •

The first day of our Metz mission dawned clear and blue over our Luxembourg field; which was unusual for that time of year. After another great American field breakfast, we geared up, walked out to our planes, ran through the visual check, climbed in the cockpit, and cranked over the engines. Metz was about fifty miles southeast of our field, so once we were airborne, it was a scant ten minutes until we approached the targets. We had been briefed on the positions, priorities, and likely resistance by our targets. Squadron leaders had to be exact for the mission to be successful.

Flying at twenty-eight thousand feet, I knew I had to pull a steep dive at maximum speed for the M-65s to penetrate the bunkers. The grid line (red line, or maximum airspeed) was around five hundred miles per hour, which would be pushing it since I had to pull out of the dive to avoid being hit by the blast. A couple of times during my training I experimented with the red line to see what would happen. I already described the effect of the spoiler and how it helped regain control in a dive exceeding maximum airspeed. Nothing fell off or exploded then, so I guess the same dynamics would apply with my thousand-pound bombs. As a side note, if I were as low as seven thousand feet and saw a tank below, I could roll over and hit the tank with a five-hundred-pound bomb. It was almost always a *direct* hit too, since I'd become very accurate through sheer practice. For me, hitting targets became sort of an art form. I knew when to let go of the bomb and get the hell out of there. I can say that without any pride, since I had a lot of training before I hit Europe. So, now as squadron leader, I approached Metz for the first time feeling assured I could take our planes to the max in a dive bomb. (And, I guess I got smarter as the war went on. Even our local military newspapers reported some of my hits in what I would call less-than-stellar writing, such as, "Spencer got the Tiger tank on his first pass." The articles were very short, and the guys that wrote them, well, they were not writers for sure.)

The German ground forces saw us coming long before we were overhead and opened fire. Flak guns pop-popped and shells exploded in the air, sending shrapnel everywhere. Our squadron didn't approach side-by-side, but instead blazed a trail one after the other—not so close that a plane might catch the remnants of a bomb and not so far back as to not be effective in the rapid assault. When the time was right, I rolled over, and, blinking from the sun's glint on my silver wings in the clear sky, I went directly toward the fort. The rest of the squadron followed, going straight down with a two-thirds throttle. We all lobbed our bombs at thirteen thousand feet and immediately pulled up. We had to pull up quickly since all that weight in a vertical dive could push us past the red line. By the time I pulled back on my stick, my elevation had dropped to four thousand feet from the momentum alone. With that kind of velocity, I couldn't pull up easily due to the tremendous G-force. As the plane shook from the strain, I pulled back harder on the stick until I finally leveled out. As I gained elevation, my radio crackled.

"Well, you guys hit all right, but I don't see any damage." That was the second flight, far enough behind us to avoid the collateral damage. "All you did was dust off the dirt and trees."

"Thanks, very encouraging," I radioed back.

Due to both age and design, the old forts were covered with soil, trees, and other foliage, which added more protection. Although we produced direct hits smack on the roofs, on a return fly around I couldn't see any trace of destruction. I knew we did our job, and did it well, but the lack of evidence of any damage at all was disheartening.

• • •

There's an interesting postscript though. Metz was finally captured by US forces and hostilities formally ceased on November 22. After the war, when I became a squadron commander in another unit, I came across a declassified top-secret report about the Metz bombings. It said the forts were put out of action not from frontal assault or aerial damage, but mostly because of concussion. Imagine that. We had two flights of four ships each carrying two one-thousand-pound bombs per plane. That meant a total of sixteen one-thousand-pound bombs detonated right on top of those forts. But according to the report, the men inside the bunkers weren't harmed by flying concrete or broken glass; they were put out of action because of severe concussion. Shockwaves from the bombs didn't go up; they went right down through the concrete, decimating everyone inside. Like a tank enduring a direct hit by an artillery round, their heads must have exploded from the ear-shattering blast from above. I realized our mission wasn't a failure after all.

SWEET TOOTH

Our squadron at Saint-Dizier was renowned for our scrumptious food, particularly the baked goods. The reason we were so lucky was that our chief cook had access to copious amounts of sugar. Not only was he an excellent chef, but he was also a bit of a scavenger.

With the exception of the Hawaiian sugar plantations, the United States was a net importer of the sweet stuff from places like Cuba and the Philippines. When the Philippines fell to the Japanese, the United States could barely supply enough sugar for its troops overseas, who needed the extra calories to help keep them in fighting condition. The remaining supply of sugar for US civilians was not enough to meet the demand, so price controls were put in place to avoid hoarding and to insure a minimum supply for everyone. Our government also believed (rightly so) that rapid inflation would happen with sugar prices, and who knew what else would be affected. So in early 1942, sugar became the first commodity to be rationed.

The little coupon books the government passed out allocated only so many pounds per month to each household. Lines of eager housewives formed in front of stores waiting to buy sugar. Those who defied rationing or cheated in some way were exposed in local newspapers as "breaching the rationing order." Red, white, and blue posters read, "Make this pledge: I will pay no more than top legal prices," and "I accept no rationed goods without giving up ration stamps."

As the 405th fighter squadron prepared to relocate from Picauville (the first airbase in France after D-Day) to Saint-Dizier, organizers had to send all the equipment forward to set up the base there. Flatbed trucks, trailers, and weapons carriers transported equipment and personnel from the west to the east of France. Like everything else in the war effort, they used ground transport since all the planes were required at the front lines.

En route to Saint-Dizier, the convoy took an overnight break north of Paris. Sometime after dinner, our chief cook, Sergeant Roberts, decided to take a look around a recently captured marshalling yard filled with German railroad freight cars. The Germans were in such a great hurry to get out because of our rapid advance that they left behind their supplies pretty much intact. As Roberts rolled back the doors of the freight cars, he came across two of them chock full of sugar! Now at that time in Europe, sugar was better than silver or gold; it was even better than cigarettes. When the sergeant made his discovery, he could barely contain himself. Apparently the Germans had eaten well during their occupation of France.

Our cook decided he had to have some of the sugar, so he had an idea. He found a large, wholesale bakery nearby and cut a deal with the proprietor. "Look," he said, "I've got two boxcars full of sugar, and I can let you have some of it if you help me."

"Sucre?—Sugar?" The baker's eyes widened. The Germans hadn't cared much about giving their precious sugar, or anything else, to their French hosts. "*Oui, oui, je peux vous aider*—I will help you," he said, almost falling over his fresh batch of croissants in his excitement.

"Okay then," said Sergeant Roberts, "I want you to take charge of the two carloads of sugar and bring all of it here to your shop. But you only get one carload, because I'll come back to get the other one soon. "*D'accord?*—Agreed?"

"*Oui*," replied the baker. They shook hands, and Sergeant Roberts left.

After we settled in our new accommodations in Saint-Dizier, Roberts asked me if he could take four days leave in Paris, "I want to see somebody for business that will enhance the life of our pilots."

Since I was operations officer for the squadron, I knew our cook was a good man, so I told him to do what he had to do. I arranged for him to drive one of our empty weapons carriers and he left. Four days later, he returned with the carrier piled high with sacks of sugar, at least eight hundred pounds in all. I gave him a congratulatory slap on the back when I saw it. From that day on, we feasted on special days with cakes, pies, pancakes, and anything else he could conjure up with that sugar.

St. Dizier, France, 1944

WARMING UP THE NURSES

In spite of its many good features, the P-47 didn't do so well when it came to warming up in freezing temperatures. The massive amounts of oil required for sixteen cylinders made it difficult to start, taking many cranks of the engine to get the prop going. The only remedy was a unique gadget called a *radial engine oil heater*. It worked using the same principle as an engine-block heater in midwinter Detroit, where drivers plugged it in early to let the engine heat up before starting. Similarly, the P-47's oil heater warmed up the lubricant before cranking over the engine. The gas-fired device sat on a small trailer about twice the size of an office desk, and before the pilot arrived, the ground crew attached a flexible tube from the heater to the engine hub to let it circulate, or bake, for a while.

Our creative pilots found also another use for the heater when it wasn't busy warming up oil. A contingent of around sixty Women's Army Corps nurses worked at a field hospital not far from our base. One day we thought it would be a good idea to somehow socialize with them, so a couple of our enterprising pilots sponsored a get-together for the nurses at our base. The first get-together went well, so we planned another one, and another. These events became so popular that the nurses wanted to know when the next one would be. I suppose it helped that we had all that sugar, and a fantastic cook who could prepare great pastries, and sometimes even served ice cream.

I was appointed to escort the ladies from their camp to our "officer's club" and back. I suppose the reason they picked me for this role was I never went over the top when it came to drinking. It just wasn't my style (except for those four bottles of champagne at the Moulin Rouge), although I did have a drink now and then. So taking my role seriously, I secured a driver who knew how to navigate the muddy ruts between the bases. With me sitting shotgun, we drove a six-by-six truck and let the nurses sit in the back on makeshift seats. *(This was the same model I rode in when I hitchhiked to Paris.)*

Since it was very cold in that truck, we had to do something about keeping the nurses warm if we wanted them to continue coming to our parties. That's when one of our crew chiefs came up with a truly great idea. To alleviate the cold, he borrowed one of the engine oil heaters and hauled it behind the truck. As we drove, the flexible tube normally placed on the engine hub was fed into the back of the truck, where it blew copious amounts of warm air throughout the enclosed area. It worked beautifully. The nurses got so warm they began to shed their overcoats, but nothing more. They were very pleased and quite warmed up by the time they arrived at our base.

There were some fairly large buildings around the Saint-Dizier airfield that were in good shape, so we borrowed one of them for our officer's club parties. Someone found a Victrola player and put on a few scratchy records so we could dance, which we did, often to the same song over and over again. In all, we hosted around ten parties between November and the end of January of that year. Each time, more and more nurses joined us, often requiring two or three trips in our oil-heater transports. In our estimation, it was American innovation at its best.

I must say that in the middle of that dismal, gray, French winter when the snot froze in my nostrils every time I took a breath, I had never seen women look better than some of those nurses, even when they wore their "Sunday best:" brown fatigue uniforms, trench coats, steel helmets, heavy black boots, and big red crosses on their left arms. Many of them had already served in North Africa or England, so they had done their time in the trenches, so to speak. They were all so nice and without pretense, making it a great way to celebrate life in the midst of all the chaos.

• • •

On December 16 the Germans launched a counteroffensive in the Ardennes Forest. Fighting was intense, and five days later, we flew missions as often as possible to assist our ground troops. They were nearly frozen in the record-breaking cold of that winter, but our guys put up a heroic fight. I was in command of a squadron designated Red flight #1. We took off that morning in haze that was thick as soup. Here is the debriefing summary after the mission.

```
Had    a    lot    of    trouble    contacting
"Turpentine,"    and    after    we    finally
did    contact    him,    he    sounded    phony,
so    Spencer    challenged    him.    He    failed
to    give    the    right    answer    twice,    so    we
called    "Ripsaw,"    and    he    said    we    could
bomb    Saarburg.    All    bombs    hit    in    the
area.
```

Toward the end of the mission we encountered "bandits"— Luftwaffe fighters—in our area but made no contact with them. The standing directive was our P-47s were not to engage in dogfights with the Germans because we were better equipped for close air support through bombing and strafing. The log entry of that mission concluded:

```
"In our recon area, the only thing that
moved was a cow, which we did not strafe.
Blankets of light flak was encountered
over Saarburg, but no one was hit. In
all, the mission was a milk run."
```

— 4 —

HE SHOOK HIS FIST

Regardless of the standing directive to avoid dogfights, there was one day we had no choice. It was December 27, and four flights totaling 15 planes were en route to work over the supply road between Trier, Bitburg, and Prum. I was Yellow's leader, covering the top for the three other flights, while they did the nasty work below with fifty-caliber machine guns and bombs. As top cover, we looked for anything that might come at the squadron to interfere. As we approached Bitburg at fifteen thousand feet, six bogeys came out of the northeast and jumped my squadron: three Messerschmitt 109s and three Focke-Wulf FW-190s. The Focke-Wulf FW-190s were known as the best Luftwaffe fighters in the war. They outmaneuvered us with speeds matching the P-47s, and capable of a greater range. There were also twice as many planes as our flight, since one of our planes had developed engine trouble and returned to the base. When we saw them coming, I informed the rest of the squadron and we lined up our flight: three planes abreast of each other.

We formed a horizontal, wing-to-wing formation and went straight for the oncoming planes. The maneuver was designed to confuse their attack, and though I'd never done it before, it made sense. We simultaneously fired all twenty-four of our fifty-calibers at nine hundred rounds per minute, which set up a wide, formidable wall of pure lead that they couldn't penetrate. It worked, and they all scattered. Then for some unknown reason, three of them broke off and left the area, leaving us to fight one-on-one. Maybe they knew they could outmaneuver us and sent the rest of the planes to find other targets. We each picked an adversary and went after him.

Since I had to climb up to meet him, the one I engaged already had an altitude and speed advantage over me. When he saw me approach, he went into a dive to pursue me, but he came down too fast and overshot my position, allowing me to countermaneuver. I jerked to the left and spun around to gain the advantage. That placed the two of us in a Luftbury circle—an inevitable cycle of constricted turns, where one plane tries to climb on the other's tail for a good shot. Temporarily in control, I zeroed in for a hit, but it was like trying to shoot a duck in flight. As soon as I had him in my sights, he went into a tight turn that I couldn't duplicate. I had to find that split second when I could open fire at close range. I tried to follow him, but my plane was far heavier than his. I couldn't keep up with his light, nimble aircraft. Before I knew it, he was behind me and closing in on me fast. Throttle full forward, I flew balls-out, but he was still getting closer to me. Soon he'd be able get a good shot. My mind raced. I had to do something dramatic, and then, in a flickering moment, I knew exactly what to do.

Back in Louisiana, before I shipped out to England, a test pilot for Republic Aircraft—the company that builds P-47s—told a few of us about one of the plane's unique capabilities. "This is probably beyond what they taught you in flight school," he said, "and very few pilots have used it to my knowledge."

After his lecture, I pulled him aside and asked him for more detail. He obliged. Now I knew if I were ever going to shake that German off my tail, I would have to put it into practice.

Reaching down to the throttle module, I adjusted the pitch of the propeller to power mode. Then I pushed the throttle full forward and simultaneously pulled the stick back for a straight-up climb. Like a power prop on a boat, the reduced pitch of my propeller moved faster as it lifted me higher and higher. I temporarily defied gravity as my plane pointed straight up at the sun. Like a dog jumping at the tail of a cat clinging to the draperies, the confused German pilot furiously tried to get a shot at me. Only the P-47, with its unique capability, could maintain that kind of game. It was my only advantage at that point. As my engine whined, I slowly climbed higher until I couldn't rise any more, suspended in midair as if by an invisible thread. I doubt that pilot had ever seen anything like it. I knew I couldn't remain in what amounted to a controlled vertical stall forever and hoped it would be enough to discourage him.

My adversary knew that in spite of his speed, my unusual position would never allow him to climb on my tail. So he finally peeled off and went into a dive, apparently unaware that nothing in the sky could dive a P-47. When I saw him leave, I readjusted to a speed pitch, shoved the stick forward, gave it a hard left rudder, and fell into a fast dive right behind him. Since his speed was greater than mine, I kicked in the water injection, and the engine surged with more power. Starting at seventeen thousand feet, we plummeted straight down. Clouds and sky whirred past us, and the world went upside down. I felt the temperature change with each thermocline as we plunged further. Right when I thought he'd dive straight into the forest, he leveled out, barely skimming the tops of the trees. I had to give him credit for that one.

I know how to do that stuff! I thought. *I've been cleaning rooftops with this thing for months.* I started to close on him since I just came out of a dive and still had good speed, but when I leveled off, I could no longer gain on him. Our planes both had essentially the same power plants, and I knew if I didn't do something soon, I'd lose the advantage. Still scraping the trees, he was at least a thousand feet ahead of me. I raised my nose a bit and let go with a few bursts of my fifty-calibers, to see if I could lob a few in his direction, but I was losing him. *(I had a good idea about leading a target since my skeet shooting days. Not many people have an award for scoring twenty-six shots without missing one.)*

The first salvo showed no result. I adjusted my lead downward somewhat and fired again until I saw what I needed. Several shards of aluminum burst from his vertical stabilizer, enough of a wound to turn the chase into a kill. The disrupted airflow caused him to lose airspeed, and he must have known the game was over. It was just a matter of time now, and I prepared for another burst, but before I pressed the button, he quickly rolled over and popped his canopy. I watched his body hurl from the cockpit toward the forest. Seconds later, his chute deployed.

As he drifted earthward, his plane made a slow arc toward the forest and disappeared into the trees. By the time it went down, I already passed it, so I didn't know if it exploded or just broke apart. Then I turned my attention back to the pilot. This was my first aerial engagement in the war, and I wanted to make the most of it.

The accepted conventions of war prevented a combatant from shooting a man in a parachute. We all knew the Germans didn't care much about such conventions, but nevertheless I knew I would never shoot a guy like that. Instead, I closed the guns down and activated the plane's camera so I could take plenty of photos of my "kill." As he slowly drifted earthward, I circled around a couple of times and captured some great photos. The third time, I came in very close and watched him as he raised his fist and shook it at me.

"Don't worry," I muttered, "I'm not going to shoot you."

I didn't want to hang around to see if he was captured by our forces, so I turned around to check on the rest of my guys. They were all okay, and when we lined up, we called it a day, and headed back to the base. After the debriefing, I read the report, written in its usual dry, clipped style.

```
December 27, 1944
We were approaching Bitburg when the
squadron was jumped by three FW190s.
Yellow leader shot down one FW, but
the rest got away. There were so many
damned planes in that area that you
could hardly move: 51s, 38s, 47s, and
a few others. Ripsaw reported 100-plus
bandits in our area, but we couldn't
make contact. Dammit.
```

Later on in the chow hall, I thought about that guy in the parachute. American fighter pilots, at least in my squadron, could kill the enemy pilot in his plane, or he might die in a ball of flames on the ground, but shooting him after he lost the fight wasn't our job. At the time, a story circulated about a German fighter who found one of our B-17s over German territory in France. The German came alongside and saw that the B-17 was badly shot up and was obviously trying to make it home. As the story went, the German fighter could easily have shot down the B-17 and gotten credit for a kill, but he could see most of the gunners inside the plane were already dead. Instead of attacking, he just flew alongside for a while. No one could read his mind, but after the fact, it looked like the German protected that B-17 from further harm, as if he had decided to help the pilot rather than kill him. Why would he do that? The answer might be a certain degree of respect among pilots, regardless of their allegiance, but I can't be sure. Pilots throughout the world go through a hell of a lot of training, and maybe that's what he had in mind. Or maybe he realized the war didn't justify killing that poor guy trying to get back to his family. Taking it further, maybe he realized the plane and its crew were no longer a threat, and the defeated pilot might transport his dead crewmen back to their base so they could be properly buried by their loved ones. Of course, that is all speculation. But for me, shooting that German plane down was my one and only air engagement in the entire war, and I was damned glad I had that opportunity.

5

NEXT STOP, BELGIUM

At the time, I couldn't compare my experience at the Saint-Dizier airfield with any other, but in hindsight it was my best experience of the war in terms of creature comforts, safety, and a good airstrip. After our squadron flew nearly forty missions, we received orders to move to our next stop, a base in Belgium named Ophoven. The order was not unexpected, since Patton finally captured the forts at Metz and was again on the move. We had to keep as close to him as possible.

The Germans still held the areas on the eastern side of the Rhine, so there were many targets for us to bomb. Several of our missions took us south to Strasburg, France, and north to Cologne, Germany, where I could see the tall, Gothic spires of the cathedrals. In fact, those spires served me well as a navigation aid in the same way a radio tower guides a ship to port. When I led a squadron, I frequently directed a safe heading back to the base using the spires as a focal point. That became routine since P-47s didn't have much in the way of navigation instruments.

We also operated throughout the northern half of France, Belgium, and the Netherlands as our armies continued to move in and set these countries free. Countless battles had destroyed everything that was destroyable, and we certainly did our part from the air. Not long after our forces crossed the Siegfried Line, General Patton and the other commanders were dying to figure out how to cross the Rhine River (The Siegfried Line was built between 1938 and 1940, and consisted of 18,000 pillboxes and tank traps. The fortifications ran from the western border of Germany across 390 miles from Kleve, near the Dutch border, all the way to the Rhine River near Switzerland). Most of the bridges had been blown up by the Germans when they retreated, and the question was how to get men and munitions on the east side of the river. Once there, the path to Berlin, and Hitler, would be far easier.

On February 14, just a few days after we moved to Ophoven, our flight was surprised by that flak train that shot me all up. That's when the Higher Power told me to switch to the auxiliary fuel tank.

GETTING TO KNOW HER AND MYSELF

Casey and I wrote each other at least twice every month. I tried not to write about the war. In fact, the army prohibited us from writing anything about what we did or where we were. Originally, it was the responsibility of the unit officers to censor their troop's communications. Before the letter went into the mail sack, they checked every page looking for anything of value to the enemy, such as our location, troop strength, even words that could hint of low morale. The unit officers hated the job, however, since it tended to create mistrust. Eventually the task went to the chaplain or the dentist.

Casey and I mostly wrote about our future: what we would do if we were married and how we wanted to live. We also wrote about philosophy, politics, psychology, and many other things not usually talked about on a date back in the States. As the letters came and went, I felt like I knew her fairly well, even if we had only spent a total of seven days together in person. We also got to know each in ways that wouldn't have been possible if we had seen each other every day. Our mail relationship was unromantic in a way, without the distractions of the physical presence. Because there was little to protect, in that sense, we dared to say things we wouldn't otherwise say in person. More thought went into our words, and I was careful to phrase my thoughts exactly as I intended. Sometimes I took hours to write a few important things, but what I said was exactly what I meant, and in a much more transparent way. The war was stressful for sure, but in the midst of it all, her words made some of my quiet times very joyful.

SNEAKY SMART AND DAMN COMPETENT

People have asked me if I was ever afraid during the war. Well, I was concerned about my health of course, like everyone else, but seldom did I experience actual fear or terror, except when my plane was hit by that surprise flak train. Even in cases like that, though, I usually regained my composure and got back to the base okay.

I tend to relate fear with risk taking, which I am not prone to do. If a person takes risks, it means they haven't prepared for the unknown consequences. I have always tried to be ready for most anything. I didn't consider flying a P-47 in combat as much of a risk since I had so many hours of training. I knew as well as anyone what I was doing up there, and I knew how to take care of myself if something went wrong. When I thought about it, my habit of being prepared, and my mentality of fending for myself started at a young age in Pennsylvania when I'd disappear for a couple of days to go hunting with my dog, Ludi. It was an adventure, and also a bit threatening because there were snakes, and a few wild animals like Black Bears. I guess those times alone in the wilderness were the closest thing to fear

I ever knew at the time. Or was it really a sense of excitement, not fear? If I measure the perception of fear I had then with flying a P-47 in enemy territory, I'd say they were about the same. Maybe that's because I never intentionally did something I wasn't sure of, and such assurance helped me stay within my limits.

I found that combat pilots in general have a good handle over the emotion of fear. If we did not, we wouldn't do what we do. We cannot be efficient in battle situations if we're overcome by fear—not for ourselves and not for our wing men. Combat pilots are a special breed, if I may say so, because when we're flying we're not anywhere else but in the moment inside the cockpit. Which is another attribute of pilots: we have a high capacity for compartmentalization, meaning we can block out everything else going on in our lives when we focus on our mission. Here's something a former fighter pilot named David Smith wrote about our genre. It sums up how I feel:

> When you are flying, you are totally focused on the task at hand. It's like nothing else you will ever do. They (fighter pilots) flew planes that leaked, that smoked, that broke, that couldn't turn, that burned fuel too fast, and with systems that were archaic compared to today's new generation of aircraft. But, a closer look might show that every guy in the room was sneaky smart and damn competent, and brutally handsome in their own way. They hated to lose or fail to accomplish the mission and seldom did. They were the laziest guys on the planet until challenged, and then they would do anything to win. They would fly with wing tips overlapped at night through the worst weather with only a little formation light to hold on to, knowing their flight lead would get them on the ground safely. They would fight in the air knowing the greatest risk and fear was that another

friendly fighter would arrive at the same enemy six o'clock position as they did. They would fly in harm's way and act nonchalant, as if to challenge the grim reaper himself.

When we flew to another base, we proclaimed we were the best as soon as we landed. Often we weren't invited back. When we went into an officer's club we owned the bar. We were lucky to be the best of the best in the military. We knew it, and so did others. One thing I know is that I was part of a special, really talented bunch of guys doing something dangerous and doing it better than most, flying the most beautiful, ugly, noisy, solid aircraft ever built and supported by loyal ground crews fully committed to making sure we came home alive.

If this looks like fighter pilots believe we're set apart from the rest of humanity, that's right. We're a special breed, not because we think we have unique skill sets, are endowed with superior intellect, or possess a high degree of courage. We're just human beings who sometime in our past lay on our backs watching clouds drift by, dreaming of being up there someday doing something good. We're consumed by the freedom, the aerodynamics, the power, and the romance of blasting through the sky in a powerful war machine.

Later in the war, however, I think I came to a point where I loved being a fighter pilot a bit too much. I'd just returned from R & R on the French Riviera, my first vacation in a very long time. A few of us flew there in a C-47 transport and stayed in a wonderful hotel named the Martinez, about two hundred feet from the shores of the Mediterranean. For eleven days we ate well, slept well, bathed every day, and met a lot of great people. While there, I had a chance to ponder what I did in the war effort. My thoughts crystallized after I returned to the base and wrote this letter:

March 16, 1945

Dear Mom and Dad,

It would be a lie if I were to tell you I wanted to stay
here until the war is over, and equally as false to tell you
I don't anticipate each mission. I can't explain what it is
that makes combat interesting. I detest killing another man
even though I can't see the bombs or fifty-caliber shells
actually do the killing. Please don't misunderstand what I'm
saying. I'm only attempting to picture what a fighter pilot
thinks of. We fight to go on every mission, fully realizing
the dangers we may encounter and the destruction we cause.
We justify ourselves by recalling what the Germans did to
their conquered countries. Yet, I secretly wonder if this is
justification.

Love, Howard

Although it was rare, once in a while some pilots had to back away from flying, although the reason was never because of fear. One of my fellow pilots got a load of flak in his ass while we were on a routine search-and-destroy mission near the Rhine River. The Jerrys opened up with their twenty-millimeter flak guns and peppered my squadron. We all got the hell out of there intact except Allen. A big chunk of shrapnel penetrated the bottom of his fuselage, passed right through his seat, and went straight to his butt. He bled a lot, and of course he was worried about the rest of his anatomy. After he checked himself thoroughly, he was assured all was good and concentrated on flying back to the field. Immediately after he powered off, the medics helped him out of the cockpit and drove him to the infirmary.

He was in the hospital around five weeks until they pronounced him good enough to return to the squadron. On his first mission out, the Jerrys opened up with their flak guns again. One of the shells exploded behind his canopy, sending several chunks of shrapnel into his back. There was less blood this time, but his wounds were more serious. The rest of our flight stuck close to him until we were assured he could make it back to the base. Upon discharge from the hospital—the second time in three months—he walked into the squadron commander's tent and said, "I can't do it again." The commander replied, "That's okay, we don't expect you to."

That wasn't a declaration of fear on Allen's part; it was the smart thing to do because the odds were he wouldn't be so lucky the next time. All of us agreed, and they sent him home.

I don't know of anyone who backed away from a mission because of fear. In fact, the only time a guy had to return to base early for something other than being shot up was if he had the shits. Whether the cause was bad food or a sudden virus, it was legitimate. When that happened, everything broke loose and it got real messy. No one can concentrate on dropping a bomb or strafing a target if he's wallowing in his own sludge. Fortunately, I never had the experience. Taking a pee in flight was another matter.

IN-FLIGHT CONVENIENCES

Our planes were equipped with a special device to assist one of our bodily functions, the need to urinate. Drawing from their wisdom and foresight, the designers of the P-47 came up with a little funnel that looked like the bottom half of an ice cream cone. It was attached to a rubber tube, and you had to pull the funnel up to the "little guy" and aim it just so and hope you hit the mark. Fortunately it was big enough for mine, but some guys who were heavy-hung might have had a little trouble with their aim.

While the device usually worked, there was always a problem of access. Whether at five thousand feet or twenty thousand feet, it was cold, and along with the cold came the natural retreat of the little guy, as if hibernating in the only warm spot on the plane. Getting to him through all the fastenings, layers of clothing, and safety belts wasn't easy. Unfortunately, the greater the urge, the harder I tried, and the more I fumbled. Try keeping an eye on formation and enemy ground fire, or bogeys, while working the rudders with your feet and the stick with one hand while keeping the other stick pointed at that ice cream cone in just the right spot. The plane would go into all sorts of gyrations, and when it happened to someone else it was hilarious. Everybody in the squadron had a good laugh when they saw it. "Hey, look at Blue four out there," someone would say. They all watched my plane wobble up and down while I did my duty. "Hey, Spence, having a good time with your boyfriend?" Of course the airwaves crackled with the entire squadron's laughter.

It could have been worse, like the time one pilot—I'll call him Red four —had to abandon his effort half way through. His calamity was a direct result of design error. The tube attached to the funnel extended down to the cockpit floor and out to the back of the plane, where the vacuum of the passing air helped pull the stuff out and away. The design engineers hadn't calculated for air speed variation or angle, so after Red four responded to incoming enemy aircraft, he let the funnel go and quickly pulled up. When the plane went nearly vertical, all that pee still inside the tube regurgitated back out of the funnel and onto his clothing, arms, neck, and face. As awful as it was, he successfully completed his mission and landed safely, relieved but smelling like a downtown public toilet.

6

ABOUT FLAK

Our pre-mission briefings always included up-to-date information on the status of German weaponry. Even if he was rapidly losing the war, Hitler's megalomania pushed him to greater heights of denial, defiance, and weapon's technology. Among his late war developments was the V-2 "Vengeance Weapon," so-named to retaliate against Allied cities for their bombings of German cities. Starting in September 1944, the Germans launched over three thousand V-2s against Allied targets, including London, Antwerp, and Liege. The attacks killed an estimated nine thousand civilians and military personnel, including twelve thousand forced laborers and concentration camp prisoners who produced the weapons.

While the V-2 didn't affect our missions that much, other German technology did. As the war dragged on, the effectiveness of flak, or "Ack-Ack guns" as they were called due to the sound they made, improved with time. Starting in late 1943 German air defenses were equipped with new, efficient radar systems. When Allied aircraft approached, the radar gave precise information on position, altitude, and number of planes. The data were processed through a "director" in the system and gave feedback about muzzle velocity, ambient temperature, wind direction, speed, etc. The information directed their gunners to calibrate bearing, fuse setting, and gun elevation.

These radar systems might have changed the course of the war—or at least the air war—but that didn't happen. The problem was dead time: the number of minutes or seconds between receiving the data and calibrating the guns. By the time the Germans pulled the trigger, the situation had changed. By then, Allied formations might have spread out, gone into a dive, peeled away, or began strafing and bombing. Nevertheless, the weapons' net gain was greater accuracy, which accounted for so many of our casualties.

If dead time decreased the weapons' effectiveness, other developments compensated for it. When the Germans sighted Allied aircraft, they fired three or four guns in salvoes to explode within a radius of sixty yards around a target. With each burst area spaced appropriately, the scope of potential damage was lethal. As time wore on, their guns and shells became larger and more powerful, such as the eighty-eight caliber, the 105 mm, then 128 mm. They sent projectiles as far as twenty thousand feet with enough accuracy to knock out an aircraft within thirty yards of the burst. However, it was shrapnel which inflicted serious damage within two hundred yards and accounted for so many of the 405th casualties.

How did the Germans manage the exact time of a shell burst? One answer was the development of the "proximity fuse," which contained its own radio transmitter. The fuse sent a continuous signal in the direction of the target as it flew through the air. Echoes bouncing back from the plane were measured by the radio, and when the echo frequency reached a certain tempo: *Boom!* It was the same technology used in radar and sonar. In 1944 alone, flak accounted for the destruction of 3,501 American planes.

As the war progressed, what helped us overcome the flak threat was dwindling German manpower. We continued to pummel their armies, and as the constant demand for German front- line troops removed well-trained flak gunners, they replaced them with elderly men, schoolboys, and even POWs. Nevertheless, the Germans of

World War II were a clever, industrious, and formidable enemy. In the face of their rocketry, radar, and other technology advances, maybe our simple P-47 Thunderbolts shouldn't have done the job, but they did, because the P-47 was a tough, durable fighter, flown by the world's best-trained, highly talented pilots.

THE BULGE

On December 16, 1944, the Germans had launched a surprise attack across a weak Allied front spanning parts of Belgium, France, and Luxembourg. They caught our forces completely unprepared. One reason the Germans successfully surprised us was poor aerial reconnaissance on our part due to lousy weather. By that point in the war, our air power was vastly superior to what was left of the German Luftwaffe, but unfortunately our squadrons were often grounded due to bad weather. We waited, helpless and unable to assist, while our guys on the ground either died in battle or literally froze to death. Whenever the weather cleared, even if only barely enough to fly, we always went out to find targets. It was difficult to judge the right target in the brief clarity because of the cloud cover, fog, or snow, however.

On the ground and in the air, our efforts were stalled by snow, sleet, fog, and wind. General Patton's frustration with the weather, compounded by the Germans taking the Allied forces by surprise, was recorded in a letter Patton wrote to God. Here is part of his transcript, which was reprinted after the war:

> *"Lord, this is Patton speaking to you. The last two weeks were steps on our way to hell. Rain, snow, more rain and still snow. I wonder, in vain, what's going on in your Headquarters. On which side do you really stand? . . . My army is not conditioned to endure a winter campaign.*

And you know that this climate is much more convenient
for Eskimos than for the Southern States Riders whom I
command. . . . Lord, I am not unreasonable. I don't ask
for impossible things. I don't want to perform a miracle.
All I'm asking for is four days of clear weather. Consent
to give me as your gift of four days of blue sky, so that my
airplanes can take off, hunt, bomb, find their goals, and
annihilate them. . . . It is too much of a burden for me to
stand by powerless at the needless holocaust of our American
youth. Amen!"

In many ways, we felt the same urge to pray like Patton. Whenever there was the slightest break, we climbed in our cockpits and went aloft to see what we could do. One mission report reflected the occasional, random nature of our missions.

January 14, 1945

Was supposed to bomb a powerhouse, but "Ripsaw 3" had a higher priority target. He vectored us into the Bulge, and we found Spooner squadron bombing the same target. The roads were covered with military transports of all kinds, all heading south. We bombed one road, and all got exceptionally good hits. Light and heavy flak covered the target, so strafing was impossible. Blue flight found another convoy a few miles to the south and made one strafing pass. Lt. Torbet was hit in the engine and headed for our lines. We are not sure if he made it.

Although we had an occasional clear day, clouds moved in and out fast, and our missions were often aborted. When we could see the target, our own forces were right up next to the enemy in tight battle, so we couldn't take any chances on dropping ordnance on our own troops. We'd circle around hoping to find a window of opportunity other than the original plan. Sometimes we were in contact with the ground controller, who might say, "If you get a chance at these grid coordinates and you're clear, go ahead and try." If we couldn't, we'd have to do something else. As our mission report stated:

> January 15, 1945
>
> Weather was pretty bad over recon area, and after being vectored around for about an hour, they finally gave us a target. We bombed a wooded area that was supposed to contain tanks. No results observed. "Ripsaw" had a strafing target, but we were low on gas and came home.

The next day we got a break.

> January 16, 1945
>
> Target area had cleared up, and weather was perfect. "Ripsaw" said he had some tanks he wanted us to bomb. We couldn't find the tanks at first, so Spencer had to make four passes before he could pick them out. They were damn well hidden. Four bombs were direct hits, and two more were very close. About

```
20 strafing passes were made. We claim
three tanks destroyed, five damaged,
and one military transport destroyed.
```

BASTOGNE

As the Battle of the Bulge raged, a certain town named Bastogne became an important battleground. Seven roads winding through the densely wooded Ardennes highlands converged on Bastogne, and control of the crossroads was vital to the Germans if they wanted to maintain any momentum. By December 21, German forces had encircled the town and pinned the US 101st Airborne Division along with others inside the town. The 101st held Bastogne through Christmas, however, although conditions inside the perimeter were very tough. Most of the medical supplies and medical personnel had been killed or captured, and those poor souls remaining suffered trench foot, extreme weakness, and frostbite. Food was scarce. By December 22 artillery ammunition was restricted to ten rounds per gun per day.

Fortunately, the weather cleared the next morning, and supplies were dropped throughout that day and the three days that followed. It looked like Patton's prayer was answered. Our squadron base was within a half hour of Bastogne, so we continued to fly missions in and around the area, as weather permitted. The Germans had several flack gun batteries around the town, and although they couldn't overrun the 101st, they continued to defend Bastogne with everything they had.

Our B-26 light bomber squadrons eventually destroyed all the bridges near Bastogne except for one bridge that crossed a small river near the town. That bridge and the road to it were jammed with Germans trying to get out, and the ensuing bottleneck caused them to suffer the same fate as our 101st Division inside the town. Our squadron dropped bombs and strafed in what amounted to a real turkey shoot. There they were, all bunched together waiting for us. In spite of their flak cannons, we swooped down on them almost at our leisure. We kept it up until either weather, low fuel, or the dark of night made us head back to base. Then we did it all over again the next day until we met our objectives.

The siege of Bastogne finally ended on December 26, when General Patton's Third Army punched through the German lines and liberated the city. As the weather continued to hold, our Allied troops continued to push the Germans back toward the Seigfried Line. As they pushed, the 405th kept finding more and more targets on the ground. It seemed we came across huge concentrations of German convoys every time we went out. Our success was reflected in a happier mission report.

January 2, 1945

Good mission today. A (weather) hole opened up, and we saw Jerry convoys moving all over hell. We were close to our lines, so we checked our position to be sure. It was Jerry, so we worked them over. We claimed 60 destroyed and 40 damaged, a conservative claim. Convoy consisted of every kind of vehicle Jerry has, including tanks.

Long after the war, historians cited the official end of the Battle of the Bulge as January 25, 1945. But I already knew it from what we saw on a mission that same day.

```
Contacted "Flabby" who gave us "Ironclad"
to work with. He told us to check for
enemy activity and tanks in the Bockholz
area. Thirty military transports were
observed in and around a small woods.
All bombs but one were dropped here.
Results were exceptionally good. Many
direct hits were observed. Jerrys must
be on the run!
```

It's sad to note that the Battle of the Bulge was by far the bloodiest battle fought by the United States in World War II. Of the 610,000 Americans involved in the battle, eighty-nine-thousand were casualties with around nineteen thousand killed. That was nearly twice the number of combined Allied troops killed on D-Day.

CRIMSON PULSE

Part way through a mission over the Ardennes, my plane took a twenty-millimeter burst inside the cockpit just behind the instrument panel, about a foot away from my legs. Unsure of the extent of the damage, I pulled way up to give some space between me and the rest of the flight. The burst knocked the instrument panel out of commission, but there was little damage to the rest of the cockpit. The engine kept running, and I didn't see any damage from a 360-degree check outside. That's when I looked down at my feet and saw blood gushing all over my shoes. It pulsed, like a major artery had been cut, and blood spewed like from a hose.

"Good Lord!" I thought. "I've got to get back before I bleed to death!"

I started to bank in the direction of the base and prepared to radio my flight with the news as I looked down at my feet again and saw something strange. It was red, but it didn't really look like blood, at least not what I thought my blood should look like. I reached down and felt around both my lower legs, but I didn't find a wound. Then I raised my fingers, which were covered with sticky stuff, to my nose and sniffed. *Hydraulic fluid!* The shell hit one of the hydraulic lines pressured with red fluid, and it shot from the severed line onto my legs.

I was about to laugh with relief, when another thought struck me, "Could I still fly the plane?" There were several hydraulic lines and electric panels where the shell struck, so I asked myself, "Which hydraulic system was out of commission? Ailerons? Rudder?" I quickly checked all functions, and to my relief, all flying characteristics were sound. Apparently that ruptured line was a backup for a primary system.

Although the plane was in good shape, I wasn't. I think I lost a pound or two just thinking about it. That's one time I was scared: I really thought I was going to bleed to death. By the time I got back to the base and cleaned up, I had quite a story to tell the guys.

"Oh yeah, Spence," one said, "you were lucky all right. I'll bet you had to change your underwear too, right?"

January 31, 1945

Dear Mom and Dad,

What I had been fearing since October has finally happened. My roof leaks! It was a hurry-up job, and I was lucky it didn't happen sooner. Perhaps I can fix it if the sun ever shines, or maybe the war will be over before I get around to it. In our club, we now have coffee in the morning and evening and occasionally some bread for toast or sandwiches. Bread is rationed to each squadron, so in order to have bread in the club we have to use less in our mess hall. Everything is perfect with me, except the war is lasting too long. The food is getting better, the club is a swell place to spend my spare time and write letters, and, in general, my morale is tops. Any time you want to send more fudge, I can assure you, it won't dry out.

Love, Howard

= 7 =

THE DEATH OF MARTY LEWIS

February 16, 1945, welcomed us with a blue sky, high scattered clouds, and great visibility. That meant we could now finish off whomever or whatever was down there that still needed to be destroyed. Our squadron ate a bountiful breakfast of scrambled eggs, fried canned ham, and blueberry muffins, the latter prepared with sugar from the last bag we scavenged from that German boxcar outside of Paris. After breakfast, we gathered in the command tent for the briefing.

Our mission that day was for our sixteen aircraft to bomb a train marshalling yard west of the Rhine River. We'd already patrolled that area for six months, so we knew the lay of the land. We also knew the Germans were never far away. The target was large and would be easy to spot from a high altitude. That was all well and good, but as I walked out to my plane, I wondered why they didn't send our B-17's to do the job instead of us. I would find out why later in the day.

Pilots in most other squadrons always flew the same plane until it either wore out for various reasons or crashed. Because each pilot had his own plane, he could decorate it as he saw fit. That's why all sorts of creative works of art appeared on the fuselages below the cockpits—scantily-clad (or naked) women named "Lulu Belle," "Heavenly Body," or "Stripped for Action." The P-47s of the 405th were interchangeable, however, so we couldn't mark our own planes with personal, good-luck art work. Every time we went on a mission, I had to check my plane very carefully. I would do so anyway, but since I didn't know who flew it last or under what circumstances, I always took a slow walk around the outside to scrutinize every square foot. The Thunderbolt was rugged and sturdy, and its air-cooled radial engine could withstand a lot of damage and keep flying, but I still had to be sure. No matter how close I checked though, in the end we had to trust the integrity of the ground crew, armorers, and the crew chief.

"Is there any problem with this plane?" I asked the crew chief.

"No, Captain, this baby is ready to go, so take good care of it."

I said I would and proceeded to walk around the plane.

"Has the armorer done his job?"

"Oh yeah," he said. "He's all through. I watched him."

I knew armorers did a thorough job because they realized our lives depended on their work, but it never hurt to ask, just in case. We depended on four-hundred-plus rounds for each gun and nothing less. I wouldn't want to run out of bullets halfway through a strafing mission.

"Were there any oil leaks?" I asked, carefully looking at all the surfaces. It was far better to find something not quite right while it was on the ground rather than up in the air. He nodded. Crew chiefs had a specific inventory and knew the condition of each plane.

I paid particular attention to the bomb mounts beneath the wings because they had a nasty habit of getting hung up once in a while. If a guy said, "My bomb hung up," I always replied, "Go out and take care of it." When a five-hundred-pound bomb is released, the timing begins, and if it's still attached to the plane, we didn't want it going off in formation. First, we tried to shake it loose by doing a snap roll or some other shock maneuver to get rid of it. If that didn't work, the pilot was forced to land with the bomb attached. Once I watched a plane land with a hung bomb. Everybody took cover because we knew what a five-hundred-pound bomb could do. Fortunately he landed without blasting a crater in the runway.

After I checked the canopy for ease of opening and closing, I climbed into the cockpit, took my seat, and checked the shoulder and body straps. Those three-inch thick supports kept me firmly seated during turbulence, flak explosions, high climbs, tight turns, and fast dives. I also checked my parachute to be sure it was where it should be and ready to deploy, not that it would do me any good when I took off because the chute wouldn't open unless I was at eight thousand feet or more. This was a problem because we flew the majority of our missions at a much lower altitude. Nevertheless, I checked the toggles and buttons to be certain that the chute wouldn't open while I was in the cockpit. That had happened before with other pilots, and it was a real mess.

I patted the right side of my flight jacket—the only winter clothing I had—and felt the outline of an important item. The jacket had big inside pockets, and the one on the right held a compact kit designed to keep me alive if I went down in enemy territory. Crammed into a packet not much bigger than two packs of cigarettes was a map of Europe made of silk to withstand moisture, four days-worth of "food" capsules to keep my system going, a small box of Band-Aids, a compass the size of a fingernail, and a few other essential survival items. Theoretically, if I were captured, I could stuff some of the smaller items into a particular body orifice for future use. Theoretically again, the Germans were unlikely to find said packet in their ordinary search procedure. Who could tell, though? They were Nazis after all. Fortunately, I never had to use the packet.

Next, I looked over the instruments before cranking the engine to establish a baseline for the indicators. I paid close attention to the instruments when I was airborne, so when we attacked a target, I'd know right away if something failed and could take corrective action.

"Let's go," I called to the ground crewman. When I pressed the starter button, the prop chugged a few times until it kicked over, sending a plume of gray-blue exhaust over the canopy. I looked at the instruments again: oil pressure up, fuel gauge pointing to full, and good hydraulic pressure. The same thing happened up and down the flight line as engines roared to life. Planes shook with their enormous collective horsepower like racehorses straining at the starting gate. I gave a thumbs-up to the ground crew and pushed the throttle forward. Moments later, the 511th fighter squadron thundered down the runway and swept up into the sky.

• • •

My flight approached the target at twenty-five thousand feet. Just as I thought, even at that altitude, clear visibility made finding the marshalling yard easy. Straight ahead were dozens of tracks loaded with German boxcars, flatcars, and engines. My plane peeled off in a dive, while the rest of the flight followed in sequence, proceeding to bomb everything in sight. The run went well in spite of heavy flak, and after we had dropped half of our bomb load, we began to pull away. On the way up, I saw my wingman, Marty Lewis, slowly bank left and start to fall off. I watched him for a few seconds, expecting him to correct and come back in line, but he didn't.

"Marty, what's the matter?" I radioed.

He didn't answer and kept dropping until he went into a full dive. I yelled, "Pull out Marty. Pull out!" When he didn't respond, I figured he was either wounded or dead. A minute later, the rest of my flight circled around to see if he bailed out, but it was hard to focus with all the flak popping around us. Seeing nothing, we were forced to head back to the base. It's a terrible thing to watch a fellow pilot go down.

There was nothing any of us could do except record his position and circumstances with the slim hope that he'd be rescued. Most likely though, if he survived, he'd be captured, and who knew what the Germans would do to him. As I watched, I knew then why the B-17s weren't called in. The Germans were very protective of their marshalling yards, so when we approached, they let loose with every eight-millimeter flak cannon they had. A B-17, with its limited speed and maneuverability, would never make it. Only Thunderbolts could do the job. Marty's situation was to be expected. Flak must have put him away instantly, and I almost hoped he was already dead.

• • •

Since I led the squadron that day, it was my job to write the report. I didn't do a very good job of it, but none of us ever did. After returning from a particularly a difficult mission, no one felt like sitting down and reporting the details. But I had to, even if I waited until early the next morning to do so.

February 16, 1945

Results: Target was to hit railroads and military transports. We crossed the Rhine at Hitmar. Red flight dive-bombed a train southeast of Hitmar. Strafed 3 trains, 2 locomotives, and 10 military transports. White flight dive-bombed and strafed train at Kluppelburg, then went home with #2 and #4 low on gas. Blue flight dive-bombed a factory at Wipperfurth with excellent hits, results all bombs on the target. Then strafed 2 trains and 8 military transports in that area. White 3 got a direct hit from heavy flak and went (down) in Leverkusen (was not seen to get out).

It was the group commander's job to write to the deceased's dependents with the sad news. After he wrote it, he read it to us as a kind of eulogy. Then we all gathered in the tent and had a drink in his honor. "To Marty," we toasted. The next morning, life went on as though he hadn't been there at all. That's the way it had to be.

If that seems callous, it's understandable. Fighter pilots by the nature of their jobs need to show little emotion, which in retrospect seems a little strange. Viewing a situation like the one Marty was in from the outside is like watching a movie: there's always a lot of emotion and everyone is fully engaged. Emotional investment can be costly, however, if you're in the situation and part of the team—living, eating, and flying together and relying on each other. Of course, if a guy really needed help, we helped him all we could. If he just had a bad hit, we didn't say, "Oh how awful. I feel so sorry for him." No, instead we went out and tried to kill the guy who shot him, and then we went on with our lives. My lack of emotion sometimes surprised me, but I suppose that was how I coped with the reality of war.

I've read the writings of many philosophers, and several have alluded to the idea that strong people don't get too involved in things over which they have no control. That's the feeling I had about fighter pilots. We all missed Marty and several others, and occasionally we'd mention them, but it was never an emotional scene. I wasn't emotional when I watched him fall from the sky; it was more a sense of, "Well, I've lost a great guy." Marty had two children and a lovely wife. He had showed me their pictures, and he had often talked about them. I didn't let that eat away in my thinking, though. I only thought I lost a good pilot and coped with it.

THE FLIGHT SURGEON

I've said before there was little or no emotion when it came to losing a fellow pilot. While that's true, it was almost always a sad occasion. If we watched someone get peppered with flak and go down, we felt terrible that his life was over, but it was a momentary feeling, and we didn't dwell on it. He wouldn't go home. He wouldn't see his wife or his children again. After the toast and a few comments in the tent, there was very little discussion. One reason we may have behaved this way was that our group lost quite a few pilots in our short existence: of the one hundred or so pilots assigned to the 405th over a year and a half, we lost twenty-five—nearly four times the average of all P-47 pilots lost in the entire war.

When we lost a pilot, we usually gathered in our "officer's club" tent and brought out the beer, if we had any. If we didn't have any beer, which was usually the case, one or more of us made an appeal to our flight surgeon, a good guy named Captain Baxter, who was from San Francisco. When we had a particularly tough mission, and we were in bad shape, we tried to convince Captain Baxter to open his four-foot by two-foot locker he kept in his infirmary and pull out a bottle. It was soothing indeed to toss down a couple of tumblers of whiskey or scotch and toast our fallen friend. *(He always had good liquor.)*

If no one went down on a mission, we would still approach Captain Baxter to say we were in bad shape. He was a flexible guy after all, but he could spot a phony in a heartbeat. I know: I was often one of them. If some of the clowns in our unit put on a good act, though, Baxter relented and gave us a round just because it was a good performance. Other times though, he'd raise an eyebrow and order, "Get your asses out of my tent."

I'd like to say that there were lots of fun times with our group, but aside from dancing with those nurses in Saint-Dizier and the precious few R&Rs in Cannes or Paris, there weren't many enjoyable moments. Our lives were consumed with missions, briefings, getting enough sleep, staying healthy, and remaining alive. For my part, I never got depressed, nor did I have what people call "downers," and I never walked around wringing my hands muttering, "Oh, this war is so awful. I wish it were over." In my way of thinking, I had a job to do, and in spite of shrapnel, injuries, and even death, it was still kind of exciting. I could say that, even with the firm knowledge that I might not make it home alive. That mentality was a very helpful: a valuable dose of Grace, I believe.

February 25, 1945

Dear Mom and Dad,

Our new living quarters are quite a treat after living in a tent. We still sleep on cots and on wool blankets, but we eat at tables with clean tablecloths over them. Best of all, we are served by cute Belgian waitresses. It used to be a small hotel before we arrived. Now the Belgian government furnishes it as quarters for us.

It hit me rather hard when you wrote about Milt Hooven. I am trying to find out where he was killed so I can find his grave, but this takes time. Permission to find him will have to come from the commanding officer of his battalion.

The captaincy was very unexpected, so I thought I'd break it to you the same day. It doesn't change my duties very much, except I'll be flying more often. The more I fly, however, the sooner I shall be home. Don't expect me soon, though, because I'll be here for some time.

Love, Howard

By the time we got used to the temporary air strip in Ophoven, we were ordered to move the 405th to another airfield near a town named Kitzingen. Located in Bavaria about 180 miles southwest of Berlin, Kitzingen had been heavily damaged before it was captured by Allied ground forces in April 1945. Using German POW soldiers as workers, the Allies cleared the damaged Luftwaffe planes and land mines from the runways and readied the field for use by American aircraft. It was designated Advanced Landing Ground R-6 Kitzingen and immediately used as a resupply and casualty evacuation airfield. Shortly afterward, our Ninth Air Force 405th Fighter Group moved in with our P-47s. As it would turn out, our time in Kitzingen would not last long.

March 3, 1945

Dear Mom and Dad,

What do you think about the war's progress recently? Needless to say, it has certainly raised our morale considerably. With packages and letters arriving regularly, the end of the war in sight, and good weather most of the time, I don't have a single complaint. From the pilot's point of view, I am very happy that everything west of the Rhine River is friendly territory. It's quite a relief when returning from a mission to know that if anything happens, you can at least be sure of getting down safely.

Love, Howard

THE BRIDGE AT REMAGEN

On March 7, 1945, our squadron received a message that Patton's forces had captured a bridge over the Rhine River. When they had rushed toward the river to prepare for the crossing to the east side, they were surprised to find the Ludendorff Bridge near the town of Remagen was nearly intact. They seized the bridge with relatively little effort, and after the engineers checked the structure, they decided it was still good enough to use. Immediately, troops, tanks, and equipment began to pour across it to the other side. Later it was determined that the Ludendorff—the only remaining bridge in the area—gave us one of the greatest military advantages since D-Day, shortening the war by at least two weeks.

The Germans had wired the bridge with over six thousand pounds of demolition charges, but when they tried to blow it up, only a portion of the explosives went off. Pushed into the east, the Germans continued to use every weapon possible to finish destroying the bridge, including mortars, artillery, and barges loaded with explosives floated down the river. It was estimated that nearly four hundred different German Luftwaffe aircraft attacked the bridge over several days. In response, we positioned the largest concentration of anti-aircraft weapons ever used during World War II.

For obvious reasons, it was the job of the 405th to help protect the bridge at all costs. For over two days, we patrolled the area around Remagen with twelve planes: one flight of four stayed at twenty thousand feet, a second at twelve thousand feet, and a third at between one thousand and fifteen hundred feet. That top, middle, and bottom flight cover allowed us to see everything between the shores and on the river.

On the first day I flew at twenty thousand feet. Early in the mission, we saw a Messerschmitt Me 262 approaching on a glide path. The Messerschmitt Me 262s were the world's first operational, jet-powered, fighter aircraft, but they weren't very good at dive bombing. Instead, they "glide-bombed" at about a thirty-degree angle, hoping to get close enough to lob their bombs and get out of there. This was my first encounter with a Me 262. As it approached, I chased it by diving from twenty thousand feet to five thousand feet. When I came up and was in range for a shot, he suddenly gave the Me 262 full throttle and took off like a shot. A stream of fire spewed from his engines in a long plume and he was gone, just like that. I closed in on him at nearly five hundred miles per hour, but he must have hit six hundred miles per hour in a couple of seconds. I fired a couple of bursts at him—mostly because I was pissed off—but I'm certain it didn't hit him.

One day without warning, the Remagen Bridge collapsed. It wasn't due to any bombings or subterfuge; it just couldn't take all that weight any longer. Unfortunately it killed several men who were working there trying to locate the rest of the unexploded charges the Germans left. To make up for the loss of the bridge, the army began to ship dozens of pontoons to the site to build another temporary bridge. Although the Remagen bridge was open for us for only a few days, General Eisenhower was so pleased with the use we got out of it that he altered his final invasion plans against Berlin.

REMORSE

If you think that my experience of the war was far removed from the grit and blood experienced by the ground troops, you would be right. By the time our group flew cover for Remagen, I'd flown nearly fifty missions with very few problems except for those I already mentioned. There was another side to what I did up there that really got to me, however. It took me quite a while to admit it out loud, and I didn't do so until years after the war, but I was probably responsible for killing as many as three hundred civilians. I didn't have any way of knowing exactly how many I killed for sure, but there were many.

During the war, there were very few large cities in Luxembourg, Belgium, France, and Germany. Instead, most people lived in small villages or hamlets, with a handful of homes, farms, or dairies. They were populated by civilians taking care of life, their farm, and with a few head of cattle. Like America in that era, they were largely agrarian. Roads meandered across fields and through forests, connecting one village to the next.

One day I got the word from a controller that two enemy tanks were blocking a road in our patrol area of Luxembourg. He wanted us to go in and destroy the tanks. I believe I speak for my fellow pilots when I say we were always hesitant to pull off such a mission because of the collateral damage. Our infantry and artillery were also hesitant, since lobbing shells in a closely populated area invariably destroyed most of the village along with the tanks. That day the controller was insistent, however.

"So, can you get rid of those two tanks? They're at the intersection of the main road and a tributary, and they're holding up everything."

I said I would.

We flew around a couple of times to check it out. As squadron leader I radioed, "Let's go in, but try not to hit the houses."

We proceeded to "skip bomb," meaning we went in low and dropped the bombs over the cobblestone road. Like skipping rocks on a lake, the bombs were supposed to bounce low and proceed directly into the sides of the tanks. We had eight airplanes on that mission, but I instructed my flight to take the first pass. We flew in low to avoid flak, because wherever we found German tanks, we also got a lot of their flak.

"I'll run along the road," I radioed, "and drop my packages to destroy at least one of them."

When you push a button to release a bomb, it starts to fall, but it's still moving at the same speed as the plane when it hits the target. I released two bombs and immediately pulled up to see the damage, but I must have been too low because when I came around to look, one of the bombs I dropped flew right with me, below my left wing about thirty feet away! Apparently the bomb had ricocheted off the granite cobblestones and just took off again.

"Shit! It's armed!" I said to no one.

I jerked a hard right and peeled away as far away from that thing as possible. All the bomb needed was the scent of my air and it would go off. From thirty feet, a five-hundred-pound bomb can be extremely damaging. If I were ever scared in my job, it would have been then, because that was about the closest I ever came to being extinguished. Fortunately for me, but unfortunately for the villagers, the bomb never hit the tank, but it exploded elsewhere in the village. My guess was it went off in a dairy farm or in someone's home. We couldn't entirely control who would be killed in situations like that. Call it collateral damage, but I still knew many innocent people suffered as a result of my thumb on that button.

March 16, 1945

Dear Mom and Dad,

It would be a lie if I were to tell you I wanted to stay here until the war is over, and equally as false to tell you I don't anticipate each mission. I can't explain what it is that makes combat interesting. I detest killing another man even though I can't see the bombs or fifty- caliber shells actually do the killing. Please don't misunderstand what I'm saying. I'm only attempting to picture what a fighter pilot thinks of. We fight to go on every mission, fully realizing the dangers we may encounter and the destruction we cause. We justify ourselves by recalling what the Germans did to their conquered countries. Yet, I secretly wonder if this is justification.

Love, Howard

═ 8 ═

WHAT THE HELL, BILL!

April 14, 1945, was a hazy, unusually hot day near the Elbe River. Americans throughout the world mourned the loss of President Franklin Delano Roosevelt, who died two days earlier. Our president left pretty big shoes for Vice President Harry Truman to fill, but most of us felt he would do a good job, especially since the war was nearing its end.

We would send out three flights of four planes to rescue part of the Second Armored Division, which had established a bridgehead across the river the day before. Just when the Second Armored Division had settled in, HQ advised them that the Russians and Americans made an agreement at the Yalta conference designating the Elbe River as a definitive line that neither side could cross. The Russians got the east side, and we got the west side. There was nothing on the east side of the river anyway: no artillery, no infantry, not much of anything, so the Germans must have gone back to Berlin to fight it out with the Russians. Such were the politics of war, and I'm sure General Patton was spitting bullets when he found out. Supposedly, he had declared that he'd be in Berlin in two days or less "if it weren't for that damned agreement."

Based on that revelation, "Mellonjam" asked us to help get the Second Armored Division back to the west side. We had already bombed and strafed some other strong points on our side of the river and were ready to head back when we got the call. I radioed that we had munitions left from our mission and would be able to help.

Our artillery units were still bombing the remnants of German units nearby, and we requested they stop until our mission was complete. They did, and soon the Second Armored was safely on the other side, scratching their collective heads. "Melonjam" couldn't thank us enough for helping out. There were no other targets of opportunity that I could see, so as far as I was concerned, we could return home. I released ten of our twelve planes to head back to Kitzingen and then radioed my friend, Bill Myers.

"Stay with me, Bill. I have an idea."

"What's up, Spence?"

"I'll tell you in a second," I responded.

Sometimes when we were on patrol looking for targets of opportunity, we didn't know what we'd find until we arrived on the scene. We just flew, hoping to find something to strafe or bomb. So as the rest of the squadron returned to base, I thought there might be something we missed and wanted to take a look, just for the hell of it really. What I did next flew in the face of my unwritten policy of not taking unnecessary risks, but the idea was so compelling I couldn't ignore it. After all, Hitler was on the run, and there wasn't much left of his army, at least where we were. I had the same feeling that day as I did when I climbed on that ice floe as a kid: it was appealing in a strange sort of way. When the rest of the squadron was sufficiently out of range, I radioed again.

"What the hell, Bill, let's fly along that autobahn and see what's there."

According to our grid maps, the wide, level autobahn below us led straight to Berlin. *(The dozens of autobahns throughout Germany were Herr Hitler's only worthwhile accomplishments.)*

I took the right side of the autobahn, and Bill took the left. We flew balls-out at around three hundred feet above the ground, hoping we'd be low enough to preclude warning any ground resistance up ahead. We flew quite a ways north without encountering German troops, guns, or anything else. Chances were the Germans were concentrating on protecting Hitler deep in his bunker somewhere in the heart of the city. Suddenly on the horizon protruding above what was left of the Berlin skyline we saw the Brandenburg Gate. It was easy to spot since I'd seen photos of it in school and in recent briefings. With its six rows of columns and a massive horizontal transom topped with a statue of four straining horses pulling a chariot, it was worn, dog-eared, but unmistakable.

As we skimmed over the gutted buildings and carnage, I marveled that I actually flew over what Hitler had once proclaimed would be the gleaming new capital of his German world empire. He'd commissioned his architect, Albert Speer, to build a model of his vision, and when Speer presented it to Hitler, he called it the *Welthauptstadt Germania*. Hitler renamed it *Germania*, declaring it would become the centerpiece of the civilized world, the capstone of his thousand-year Reich.

"Okay, Bill, I think this is enough," I said, not wanting to push our luck.

We turned around and headed full throttle back toward our base, happy to get out of there. After we landed, we walked around our planes and verified what we thought: we'd both been hit. Bill had three bullet holes and I had two—each from a quick-on-the-draw infantryman's thirty-caliber rifle. He apparently saw us coming in at a low altitude and tried to shoot us down to "strike a blow for the Fuhrer."

If I had been caught, I probably would have been court-martialed for going beyond the Elbe River, since it belonged to the Russians. If Bill had been shot down someplace between the Elbe and Berlin, I likewise would have been court-martialed. There would be no way I could talk myself out of that one. But it worked out well: I didn't lose Bill, and he didn't lose me. My report was more brief than usual:

```
April 14, 1945
Results: "Melonjam" of Second Armored
said he had an urgent mission, so we
worked with him. We covered an area
southeast of Madgeburg, on the deck, so
a company of doughs that were surrounded
could withdraw—they got back across the
Elbe safely. "Melonjam" was emphatic
about his thanks. It was a good mission,
but we landed at 2110—quite dark!
```

Incidentally, Bill is still alive as of this writing. He's relaxing on a little ranch in the hills of Colorado not far from where his daughter lives. He and I talk once in a while and always laugh about that side trip to visit Hitler's broken dream.

THE PHONES WENT DEAD

"How the hell did you do that?" he asked.

My Saint-Dizier crew chief looked dumbfounded. I didn't know anything was wrong until I killed the engine and saw him standing there scratching his head. When he pointed to my wing, it looked like something with big jaws had taken a bite right out of the leading edge of the wing about ten feet from the fuselage. Then I realized I'd whacked a telephone pole right off its foundation.

It happened when we were strafing a couple of tanks along a populated area near Wurzburg. We were all out of bombs by that time in our mission, but I was unwilling to pass up a good target. Since we couldn't hit a Panzer tank head-on due to their considerable speed and heavy armor plating, we had to swoop in low and fast to hit them on their sides. My flight of four planes came in at around twenty feet off the ground going three hundred miles per hour, firing all eight of our fifty calibers, hoping to take out their treads. I must admit the effect of skimming so low at that speed was thrilling.

Hundreds of bullets fired simultaneously can have a devastating effect on most anything, including tank treads. It helped that our eight guns were calibrated to group into a circle the size of a card table at 250 yards, so when I let go with eight-hundred-plus rounds per minute, I immediately plunged a group of sixty-four bullets into the target. With each fifty-caliber bullet the size of a fountain pen and weighing as much as a fully loaded Swiss Army knife, that's a lot of destruction.

Just after I made a pass and was about to pull up, I felt the plane jerk to the left, as if something hit me. I wasn't too worried since it didn't knock me down or hurt my ability to fly. Looking back, I do recall seeing several of those poles (the Germans used telephone poles like we did back then), so I must have caught one right in the middle, shattering it like a matchstick.

My crew chief pulled out his tape measure and held it next to the bite. The indentation was fifteen inches deep and about two feet wide. When I saw that, I gained even more confidence in the P-47. It was amazing to know that with all that damage, I could still complete the mission and fly home without even knowing anything was the matter.

I LOST MY TAIL

This was another mission I'll never forget. The day was overcast and our squadron flew at a steady eighteen thousand feet as we approached the target outside of Bitburg. We were supposed to hit another marshalling yard, and I flew Blue number three. Over the chatter in my earphones and the dull roar of my engine, I heard the muffled *thump, thump* of eighty-eight millimeter shells bursting all around like popcorn in a pan without a lid. Out of my periphery I saw a shell go off; it was so close I could have touched it. Immediately a full load of shrapnel hit my plane, making it shudder with the impact. The stick wobbled a moment but then steadied. I knew I took a major hit, so I took a few seconds to assess the situation.

It looked like most of the damage was in the area around my turbocharger in front of the tail. Used for high altitudes to boost horsepower, the turbo wasn't necessary at our low level that day, so it didn't affect performance. Aside from numerous holes in the fuselage, it seemed like my plane responded the way it should. I concluded it might be another situation like that telephone pole.

Twenty minutes later we finished our mission and headed back to the base. I was in the middle of the pack when we approached the landing strip. As soon as I touched down my plane kind of shimmied in a strange way, but quickly steadied itself. After I slowed and made the turn to my spot, the plane suddenly reared back like a spooked stallion, and I heard a loud scraping noise of metal against metal. When I found myself looking straight up at the sky through my spinning prop, I immediately pulled back on the throttle and cut the engine. Several of the ground crew ran toward me waving their arms.

When I opened the canopy and looked, I saw the entire rear half of my plane sitting on the runway about a thousand feet back. It had split in two, right where the turbocharger used to be. I must have flown the rest of the mission with my tail section virtually held together with Scotch tape and rubber bands. It was another case of what must have been divine intervention, when I realized how close I had come to going down if my plane had broken apart in the air instead of on the runway.

Ordinarily our superb ground crew would get right to work fixing a plane when it returned full of holes, but that time they didn't even try. They used a pushback vehicle to move my plane off to the side, and as far as I know it stayed there for the remainder of the war.

JUST TAKE THE AUTOBAHN

If a plane gets shot up, a competent pilot can land his plane in a field with his wheels up. That happened a lot during the war, and again it was the P-47's sturdy construction that made this possible. We had a couple of choices if such an event occurred. First, if there's a fire on board, the pilot could crash land with a "slip" maneuver, placing the aircraft in a sideways slip to force the flames away from the pilot. Another is if the pilot had no control over the plane, he could crash as quickly as possible and hopefully get out in one piece. The third option was bailing out, which was almost always out of the question since we were usually low-flying attack planes with insufficient altitude to deploy a parachute. Finally, in a really bad situation with no chance to slip, crash, or bail, the pilot was usually gone before he hit the ground anyway.

In March 1945 our squadron got beat up pretty badly, and one of our planes had to crash land. Fortunately we were close to one of the many autobahns in the area, so we gathered around the stricken plane to protect him from any Germans lurking in the woods. Autobahns were wide enough for landings, and they all had nice surfaces, far better than our makeshift, punched-steel runways back at the base. It was fairly cold as usual, but there was no snow or ice on the road to complicate the landing. We heavily strafed the area where the pilot wanted to land and stayed close by while he went in.

When he hit the ground his plane didn't catch fire, although smoke poured from his engine. We saw him climb out of the cockpit and hold his arms high indicating, "I'm okay." Then he waited while we circled around, knowing he'd be all right as long as the Jerrys didn't show up. We kept circling and strafing until we were certain there was no danger, and then one of our planes landed. He taxied to where the downed pilot stood and cut his engine. When he climbed in, the plane spun on its tail, revved up, and took off with the downed pilot seated on the other pilot's lap.

Our P-47s were known as one of the most comfortable cockpits of its type, so there was enough room for the two, cozy as it may have been. Circling a thousand feet above, I watched the whole thing and thought it was pretty cool.

A SORROWFUL MISSION

It was inevitable. We all knew it would end sometime soon. On April 22 the Red Army took Berlin at the same time our Allied troops marched into Czechoslovakia. On the April 25 the US Army and Red Army linked up at Torgau on the Elbe River. Then on April 29 German armies in northern Italy surrendered. When we heard this news, we certainly rejoiced, but the war had dragged on for so long that anything short of a full cease-fire didn't mean a lot to us. For the 405th Fighter Group, these events had little effect on our daily lives. According to the mission report, it was business as usual, with a twist.

```
            April 29, 1945
Flew our first mission from R6. Also
was our first trip over Czechoslovakia.
Had a recon in the Pilsen area (where
we heard good beer is made), in Prague,
and in the Karlsbad area. It was quite
a thrill to be working with "Ripsaw"
```

```
again and trying to keep up with "Blood
& Guts." White and Blue hit a yard at
Beroun. We then looked at Prague (nice
airport). White flight then hit three
virgin trains at Krocehlavy. White 2
said he was hit by small arms fire, but
(it turned out later) he had a hole as
big as a bucket in his fuselage. Saw a
large refugee train at Waldsassen. This
country is piss-poor for navigation.
```

On April 30, Hitler committed suicide in his Berlin bunker, two days after Mussolini had been captured by Italian partisans and hanged. On May 2, our Second Armored Division captured Berchtesgaden and Hitler's infamous Eagle's Nest. Like dominoes, German armies surrendered in Denmark, the Netherlands, and northern Germany. Admiral Donitz, successor to Hitler after his death, sent a delegation to Eisenhower's headquarters in Reims to discuss terms of surrender. Then on May 6, General Jodl, Commanding Officer of the German forces, arrived at Reims to begin negotiating the German capitulation. At 2:41 a.m. on May 7, the unconditional surrender of Germany was signed in Reims. By then, Allied forces and the 405th Fighter Squadron understood the lengths to which Hitler went to force his dreams on innocent people.

```
            May 7, 1945
Results: Mission was a demonstration
flight over prison camps in the area
southwest of Linz to let the POWs know
they were under aerial observation—
morale flights. Beautiful clouds but
too many of them were over the area.
```

```
We also saw the Alps from 14,000
feet, and we weren't very high above
them. Overcast prevented our reaching
the target. Checked our new home at
Straubing, Germany.
```

That sanitized, post mission report did not address the horror of the prison camps we flew over. Following the Soviet liberation of Auschwitz in early 1945, more and more prison camps were revealed, exposing the sickening obscenity of the Holocaust. Had I or anyone else in my squadron known what those camps really looked like, or how so many had died at the hand of the SS, I'm sure the report would have been more compassionate. As it was, reports of the genocide would trickle out as our ground troops assessed how much the mighty *Fuhrer* had wrought.

That was my last mission in the war. On May 8 at 3:00 p.m., victory in Europe was officially proclaimed, and the Allied countries across Europe celebrated.

May 11, 1945

Dear Mom and Dad,

As they say over here, La guerre est finie. (The war is over.) Now I'm curious as to what they intend to do with me. It will be one of three things: either I shall remain here as part of the occupation force, or I shall return to the States as an instructor, or I shall go to the Pacific theater of war. Whatever is decided, I won't kick because the war hasn't been too rough for me so far.

It has been over a month since I have received any mail, but our recent move from Belgium to Germany is the reason. Germany gets more beautiful every day, and there is nothing we can do to enjoy it. We can't leave the base, we can't, and do not want to, fraternize with the Germans, and it is very difficult to get any leaves in England, France, or Belgium. There was no celebrating done over here, and strangely enough I'm not nearly as happy as I thought I'd be. As far as I'm concerned, the war is still going on. I hate the Germans; I'm in the army, and every regulation is in effect, so the only difference is that I'm not flying missions. As soon as I find out something, I'll let you know, but until then, just be patient and curious, as I am.

Love, Howard

≡ 9 ≡

I'LL GO WHERE THEY WANT ME

When the actual fighting stopped, the 405th moved from Ophoven to our final European base near Linz, Austria, not far from the Danube River. Our squadron was earmarked for transfer to the Pacific, so we spent several weeks undergoing further training and indoctrination. But we knew the fall of the Japanese empire was imminent and that the Japanese would go the way of the Nazis.

Although we planned for a possible trip to the Pacific, many of us began to think about life after the war. Between classes I asked for advice from some of the older members of our group. The flight surgeon was very especially helpful. All of them encouraged me to take advantage of a free college tuition plan from the government, later known as the GI Bill. I made my plans accordingly.

June 9, 1945

Dear Mom and Dad,

I know what you want to hear, but I can't tell you. We still don't know if we're coming home, staying here, or going to the Pacific. Whatever is decided is all right with me. More than anything, I want the war completed so I can come home. So as long as I can help, I'll stay where they want me. No doubt you are quite aware that Casey and I

have some big plans for the near future. We aren't engaged,
and I haven't proposed directly, but it won't take me long if
I get back home.

In the last month I have seen Lake Constance, Lake
Geneva in Switzerland, Lyon, France, Brussels, all of
Germany, parts of Austria and Czechoslovakia, Paris,
Luxembourg, and nearly all of the Rhine River from Basil,
Switzerland, to the North Sea. Last night a few of us found
a hospital unit about five miles from our base, so for a
welcome change we talked to American girls.

Love, Howard

I was indeed fortunate to be able to see several countries in Europe during the war, and even more after the victory in Europe. If there was any country I absolutely loved, it was Switzerland. That was the most enjoyable and unusual vacation I could remember at the time. A bunch of us took a transport to the town of Lucerne, on the edge of a lake with the same name. I thought it was the most beautiful place I'd ever seen. On the third day we traveled to Interlochen, where we stayed at the Gstaad, a famous winter resort. The next morning I walked to the top of a mountain and beheld a panorama so beautiful it was hard to describe. We went on to Lake Geneva, then Lausanne, and finally to Basil, near the French-Swiss border, where we spent our last night.

The Swiss were extremely friendly and generous, going out of their way to help us have a good time. They even invited us into their homes and bought small gifts for us. The entire country was cleaner and neater than any other European nation could ever hope to be. All their railways were electrified, and even the small chalets on the mountainsides had electricity and telephones. There was no illiteracy, and the homes were as modern as their cities, often making our own country look old-fashioned in comparison. Finally, I found the Swiss women to be attractive, and they even dressed like American girls. I don't know if my perspective was all that accurate, or merely a reaction to long months away from women in general. Regardless, I was so impressed that I decided I'd like to live there for a few years.

• • •

On August 6, 1945, we dropped the first atom bomb on Hiroshima. Three days later, a second was dropped over Nagasaki. Japan surrendered on August 15th, an then on September 2, 1945, the world watched while the Japanese emperor signed an unconditional surrender with General McArthur on board the *USS Missouri*. That was good news for all of us of course, but we of the 405th didn't necessarily throw our hats in the air and cheer. Instead, our reaction was somewhat subdued. I suppose the reason we didn't show any emotion came from many months of our disciplined calm, essential for pulling off successful missions and for our very survival. We learned how to quash our passions quite effectively, so that when there was any cause for elation, we didn't know how to show it. As I ponder that period of my life, I conclude that fighter pilots are the most unemotional people I've ever encountered.

The War Department decided there was no need to ship us to the Pacific and told us we would soon board a transport for home. Of course, everyone felt relief that we would soon be with our families, but the feeling was internal. Just like with the news of the victories in Europe and the Pacific, there were no shouts of joy in my squadron: we just processed the information.

I guess I felt let down. The joy of flight for its own sake, combined with the adrenalin rush and split-second reactions in combat, had become a daily regimen. When it all stopped, I felt like I'd lost something. I know I wasn't the only one; I could see it in the eyes of my fellow pilots when we toasted the news with a drink. All the cheering happened back in our cities, towns, and our homes. For us, unraveling the caution and self-preservation forged through constant threat of death would take time.

The plan was to wait in Marseille, France, for orders to be shipped back to the States, so we boarded a train to Marseille and were crammed into the infamous, "Forty and Eight" boxcars. These boxcars were so short and narrow that they got their name because each one was only large enough to hold forty men or eight horses. They placed straw on the floor for us, which was a dandy little enhancement to make our journey more pleasant.

MARSEILLE

Our new home overlooking Marseille was situated on a high bluff the Army Corps had bulldozed flat enough to hold several rows of tents. It was not a very exciting home, but we thought it wouldn't be too bad since we wouldn't be there that long. The ship they promised never materialized, so we waited for the next two and a half months. Every day we hoped to see the black smoke of our transport on the horizon, but it never came. Every day they told us some baloney excuse, until we knew we'd heard them all. There we sat, eating the grit and dust blown by the constant wind. It seemed like we were the "forgotten group."

September 6, 1945

Dear Mom and Dad,

For the first time since I joined the army, I have absolutely nothing to do. We seldom eat breakfast, preferring to sleep until ten or eleven. During the afternoon we read or maybe go into town. Lately I've been playing bridge, so you can imagine how hard up we are for amusement. Nearly every night there is a movie or a USO show.

After gearing up and delivering a lot of damage to Hitler, we faced the indignity of lounging around in our tents doing absolutely nothing. We looked at each other and thought, "Well, what do we do now?" In these hours of nothingness, I thought about others who had fought and those who contributed to the war effort in other ways. I ended my letter of September 6 like this:

> *I received a letter from Bob Fredette and also one from his girl. Apparently he had rather a bad time while a prisoner of war, and he feels that he didn't do his part during the war. I hope I never meet or know anyone that holds that same opinion—I might do something I'd be sorry for. The adjustment an ex-prisoner of war must make is far greater than that of other servicemen. They need assistance and understanding, and not pity.*

> *Love, Howard*

I was never prone to depression, but I could see how someone get very down in the dumps with that kind of life. If I were a psychologist, I might have credited the army with their imposed "down time" so pilots could decompress from the intensity of long months in a war zone. However, I couldn't bring myself to believe that, since I'd experienced so many other goofs by the powers that were.

We managed to go into Marseille once in a while to break the boredom, but it was kind of a corny, seaport town, and I didn't have any great love for it. I'd experienced so much of Europe already, so to explore another city held no great interest for me. Still, it was better than sitting around tents up on the bluff breathing in all that dirt.

The army, in their infinite wisdom, decided to stop forwarding mail since we might be gone at any moment. Their solution was to have us send a letter to our parents or loved ones—a form letter, no less—telling them not to send mail. Regardless of the army's attempt at efficiency, the message came across as particularly ominous.

September 9, 1945

Dear Mom and Dad,

    Effective immediately and until further notice, please do not send any more mail to me at the address given below. I will advise you promptly when mail should be resumed and will give you my proper address. I cannot do so for military reasons.

Capt. Howard W. Spencer O-734019

One day when I least expected it, I looked to the horizon and saw those beautiful smokestacks belching black soot into the air. We were told it was our transport, but no one would believe it until we could actually touch the riveted steel of its hull. Our long wait finally over, we quickly packed our belongings and boarded a truck for the pier. Suddenly, boredom was replaced by the thrill of being homeward bound and of reuniting with families and friends many of us hadn't seen in a very long time.

In contrast to my first sea transport the year before, this journey was much slower (probably because I was anxious to get there) and somehow more relaxing. I shared a cabin with a few other officers and had access to the open deck. As I gazed out to sea, I reminded myself that there were no more German U-boats lurking beneath the waves waiting to send torpedoes our way. As I breathed the fresh sea air, I felt great pride knowing our country had accomplished a brave, monumental chapter of our history.

I also had time to ruminate about my part in the war effort and what I learned during my eight months of combat duty. I even wrote them down. These are some important things I had I learned how to do:

1. Overcome whatever fear I might have during serious situations.

2. Make quick decisions under pressure.

3. Lead people in critical, often dangerous conditions.

4. Plan my activities.

The last entry might seem obvious, but it was a valuable skill. Every mission required a specific objective with a proposed route laid out on a map, so I knew where I was going. Now that my fighter missions were over, I knew I should apply the same skill to my new life. I also realized my life was a wonderful gift because I was never wounded, taken prisoner, or killed. Now I should plan to make the most of that gift.

As the ship coursed its way to America, I also realized how fortunate I was compared to others in my squadron. During my eight months in Europe, I flew almost ninety missions, one mission every three days, on average. Most of my missions were very short—maybe a couple of hours—because our squadron stayed close to the retreating German lines. Regardless of its length, after every mission there were a few holes or other damage in the planes, and, for some reason, my plane received the lion's share. I went through four aircraft in eight months, destroying them to the extent they were only good for scrap.

My service with the 405th started at our base in Saint-Dizier, France. Then I was at bases in Ophoven, Belgium; Kitzingen, Germany; and finally, Straubing, Germany, near the Danube River. Between April 1944 and May 1945, the 405th Fighter Group lost 125 P-47s with another seven hundred severely damaged by flak. Sixty-nine of our pilots were killed in action.

Part IV

A NEW FLIGHT PLAN

December, 1945 – 2008

≡ 1 ≡

MR. SPENCER

We docked in New York and immediately caught a train to an army base in New Jersey. Ingloriously named Camp Shanks, the base served as the army's out-processing center for service members returning from the war.

If there was an issue or possibility of staying in the army, no one spoke about it. Nor did anyone come to me and say, "Mike, would you like to stay in the army?" If they had, I would have given them a flat no! There wasn't any money to be made in the army, aside from our meager base pay and the $250 flight pay a month. I already decided I could make more money and have a better life as a civilian than I ever would in the military. Besides, I didn't like the military anyway : they always told me what to do, where to go, when to get up, what to wear, and how to salute. That was fine for a while because I wanted to be a part of the big thing our country was involved in, but when it was over, there was no doubt in my mind I would get out of the service. My only challenge was how I'd fit into the grand scheme of things as a former fighter pilot.

One option I considered was to become a commercial airline pilot. But I would be one of thousands of fighter or transport pilots going after the same job. At the time, commercial airlines were still in their infancy; they were a small part of the overall transportation industry in the United States. Flying was also expensive and still perceived as dangerous, so most travelers going any distance drove or took a train. Commercial airlines also needed pilots with multi-engine experience, but my experience consisted of a handful of four-engine hours in my log, aside from checking out with twin-engine bombers like the B-26. Only those with multi-engine experience were given first consideration, which would put me at the end of a long line of applicants. "Why bother?" I decided.

Another job option was to apply to the State Department, where I would be based in Washington DC and would probably travel internationally. This idea appealed to me very much, so I wrote a letter of inquiry to their personnel department, but I was disappointed when they told me how low the salary would be. That's when I decided to go back to school, find a field with some kind of future, and learn how to build or run companies. First though, I had to get out of the army.

• • •

After my discharge, I immediately went to see my parents in Youngsville. It was a joyous occasion, filled with catching up with the lives of my family and the other people in my home town. I felt like I'd gone back in time, and while everything felt the same on the surface, I knew it was very different underneath.

A week later, I told my parents I had to go see that certain girl I liked and with whom I'd corresponded for nine months. I told them she was still the one I thought I should team up with for the rest of my life. I turned to Mom, who looked slightly worried, and said, "She looks a lot like you, and I know you'll love her." Then I told my dad, "I think this is the girl I'm gonna marry, but I gotta find out if she's still there." I quickly arranged a trip to Kansas City to see Casey. I borrowed Dad's 1932 Chevrolet (he only had Chevrolets) and drove 940 miles in a little over sixteen hours to Casey's house.

I mentioned earlier that pilots in general, and me in particular, were not emotional animals, but when I saw Casey after all those months, well, it was highly emotional for both of us. I didn't shout or cry, but it was obvious she was happy to see me, and I was certainly overjoyed to see her. I told her she hadn't changed, that she was the same girl I came to know through her letters. Having written to each other for ten months in all, including my training in the United States, we had learned a lot about the other through our letters. Apparently we were both pleased with the results. I guess I was reasonably agreeable to her mom and dad too, since they insisted I stay with them instead of paying for a hotel room. They had me sleep on the sofa bed in the hallway, while Casey slept in her room. Her parents knew Casey wouldn't go for any hanky-panky, but they made sure of it by placing a lot of house between the two of us.

Two days after I arrived, I asked Casey to be my wife. She said she would, and we set the date for the following July. Then I took a bit of a risk by placing a condition on our marriage: I told her if we were going to be a successful team, I needed a full college degree in another field besides accounting. I said I hoped she would help me by going to work while I was in school. I told her about the GI Bill, that they'd pay my tuition and a small stipend, and that I'd work when I could, of course. When she agreed, I said we should get married before I started school.

• • •

My parents came out from Youngsville, and we were married in Kansas City on July 6, 1946. It was a good wedding: elaborate enough with all the things a wedding should have. Two days later, we said goodbye to Casey's family and drove with my parents back to Youngsville. Dad let me borrow his car again so we newlyweds could drive to Blue Mountain Lake in the Adirondacks of central

New York. It was a fabulous place with blue lakes, thick, green trees, and very quiet. The perfect place for a honeymoon.

Wedding day, 1946

BACK TO SCHOOL

Back in Youngsville, we spent a few days with my parents, packed our three suitcases, and caught a train for Philadelphia and the Wharton School of Business. I planned to use my accounting background to pursue industrial management and Russian studies: industrial management for practical employment and Russian studies because I thought it would be interesting.

We rented a room for thirty-five dollars per month. It was an interesting arrangement because we had to walk through the living room of the people who owned the house and take the rear stairway up to our little domicile. We had an icebox—the kind using blocks of ice delivered by the ice man—and a stove. If we wanted to get a breath of fresh air, we climbed through a window to a tarpaper roof we called our own little roof garden.

I started school and did some odd jobs when I could while Casey went to work every day as a secretary. In addition to my tuition payment from Uncle Sam, I got an additional ninety dollars per month for living expenses. It's hard to imagine today how we got by on $2,000 per year for rent, food, etc.; and the total included Casey's salary. There was no money for entertainment or anything else, but like any young couple very much in love, we had each other and the excitement of a rosy future. We lacked nothing, really.

Reassured I still had the required energy and focus, I plowed into my studies. I went all the way through without taking any summers off, finishing my undergraduate degree in three years. Looking back, we both agreed we enjoyed that time tremendously. Casey did a fabulous job and never complained. Not once.

University of Pennsylvania - Wharton School Graduation
with my Dad and Casey, 1949

THE SHADOW OF CONFLICT

Posttraumatic stress syndrome (PTSD) wasn't identified as such after World War II, but there was a lot of it going around. Everyone returned from the war ready to get on with their lives as soon as possible, so if there was a disorder of sorts it wasn't attributed to combat; it was thought to be some other kind of problem.

Although I was married, in school, and happily engaged in life, like any other person who served in the war, I experienced a certain degree of stress. I can best describe my feelings as being sort of antsy, an off-and-on sensation. I wasn't aware of it at the time, but looking back I realize it lasted around two years. Sometimes after dark, I'd walk out of the house and roam the streets for a couple of hours. It was nothing dramatic, but I didn't quite know what was going on, and I knew I was not always a happy camper. I got this antsy feeling often, but I never got depressed or let it hurt my relationship with Casey. I was just a little confused, I believe. I slept well and didn't have bad dreams, although once in a while my wife told me I woke up and mumbled something. I was fortunate that it didn't go any further than that, and after a couple of years, it disappeared.

I imagine others came back from the war with far bigger problems, and how they dealt with it I can't say. As for those in my squadron, through the years we occasionally had a reunion when we talked about the war, but not much else. One pilot, Homer, became our squadron's de facto scribe. Homer was shot down over France and spent the last two years of the war in a POW camp. When he got back to the States, he started keeping track of the rest of us. That was how I knew where they lived and who died and when.

I believe keeping track of familiar companions during a tough period of his life was how Homer managed his postwar trauma. I usually call him around Christmas time, and the last time we spoke, I asked when we'd have our next reunion. He said we probably wouldn't because he, I, and another pilot named Bill Myers were the only ones still alive. We decided that wouldn't be much of a reunion.

═ 2 ═

MY FIRST REAL JOB

I didn't waste any time looking for a job after earning my degree at Wharton. I was ready to get to work, earn good money, and take the burden of a daily job from Casey. So when the American Thread Company accepted my application, I didn't need to think it over too much. At last, I was the bread winner for my family.

My first assignment was in the production department of their Willimantic, Connecticut facility. Casey and I found a house in Windham Center, a little colonial town about three miles from my job. It was the smallest house you could imagine, with only twelve hundred square feet of living space, including the back porch. It was far better than our apartment in Philadelphia, since it had two floors and had a nice fireplace. There was even a barn in the backyard, and a large, spreading maple tree, which made a perfect spot for a patio. It was also the right place for us to start our family, and later in 1949 our daughter, Regina, was born.

• • •

Even after marriage, college, landing my first professional job, and becoming a father, I still felt the urge to climb into the cockpit of a fighter plane. It wasn't a problem so much as a desire to resume something I loved and was good at. To remedy the urge, I joined the Connecticut Air National Guard. Not only did I find my wings again, I also got some additional income, earning fifty dollars per month flying their planes on weekends. It was a true win-win for all of us, and I eventually became the squadron commander, mainly because of my accumulated flight hours in the war and my rank as captain.

JUST WHEN THINGS WERE GOING SO WELL

Shortly after our second daughter, Chris, was born in 1950, the Korean conflict broke out. A few months later, my 118th National Guard fighter squadron was called up for active duty—the first US squadron to be activated. There I was—six years after the end of World War II—back in it.

Our first base was the newly reopened Suffolk Air Force Base in New York. Our mission was to protect the US coast from New York City to eastern Massachusetts. It wasn't a glorious assignment, since we spent from eighty-five to ninety hours every week sitting in cockpits at the end of the runway waiting for orders. If there was an upside to it all, the base was near the coast, where we spent our off time fishing and having clambakes on the shore. We were a good bunch of experienced pilots who had a lot in common, which made life back in the military worthwhile.

We moved into a house in a quaint Long Island community named Quogue. The owners were a very fine Italian family, and the sweetheart grandmother sort of adopted our two daughters. That made life easier for Casey, since I was away quite a bit. Several months later, I was sent to Williams Field in Phoenix, Arizona, for several weeks of training in the new Air Force F-86 Sabre jet. When I returned to Quogue, I was told to get ready for deployment to Korea as a replacement fighter pilot. I accepted the fact that I might not only have to leave Casey again, but this time I might have to leave my children as well.

Several weeks passed without word until the spring of 1952, when I received an unusual request from the Pentagon. As commander of my squadron, they wanted me to find someone with a unique set of qualifications, including experience as a flight trainer, command expertise, and language proficiency. I thought that request was a bit strange, since it fit my qualifications to a tee. I wrote back, informing them I had found someone to meet their needs and offered to fly to Washington, DC the following week to discuss it. When I arrived at the Pentagon that Monday, I immediately became lost in the maze of hallways and offices. After what seemed like an hour of wandering around, I finally found the officer I was to report to. Colonel Andrews told me he studied my file and approved of my qualifications for the job—a special mission to organize and train the Portuguese Air Force. The colonel was a serious, uptight kind of guy, so when he finished, I cracked a joke.

"So that's kind of like training the Swiss Navy, right?" I chuckled. He didn't laugh.

"This is a very serious thing," he said.

"Yes, Sir," I replied, straightening my posture.

Then he went into detail about what I was to do. I was to be in charge of a delicate US Air Force mission, heading up a military-assistance advisory group assigned to the Portuguese to develop their air force at a location near the Pyrenees Mountains. My team would include sixteen US Air Force specialists, and I would be in charge of it. I was to complete the project within six months. I would also produce a written tactical doctrine and train pilots to a level of proficiency enabling them to man two new fighter squadrons of American-made P-47s.

As he spoke, I relaxed. I knew this was exactly what I was trained to do and that I'd do an excellent job. It was also far better than going to Korea only to be shot at again. When I got home and told Casey, she took it all in stride. After some deliberation, we decided she would take our two children to Kansas City and stay with her parents while I was abroad.

WINE BEFORE EACH MISSION

My team of specialists boarded the *USS Cowpens*, a small aircraft carrier, in New York City. Also on board were fifty P-47 fighter planes left over from the war. Coincidentally, also on *Cowpens* was a navy officer named Jack Macey, who had married my sister, Helen, shortly after I married Casey. That coincidence would make my Atlantic crossing far more enjoyable. A few days later, we set sail for Europe.

I have to say my third sea voyage across the Atlantic was far better than the first two. I had my own cabin, ate in officer's dining areas, and in general enjoyed the voyage, except I missed my family tremendously. Several weeks later our ship pulled into the Lisbon harbor. The wings of the P-47s had been removed so they could be trucked to the new airfield, and when they were back on, our squadrons were in business. Two days later, the Portuguese military hosted a reception, where we met fifty-five Portuguese student pilots. They all seemed well educated and enthusiastic, even if none of them spoke English.

We would conduct ground school, expose them to the planes, and eventually check out each student pilot's proficiency. Except for the translated training manuals and classroom instruction, the program matched the ones I taught in Yuma during the war. I wondered how effective I'd be training them in the combat tactics of the P-47 at a base up in the *Alto do Talefe* Mountains of Portugal. It would be interesting, because prior to our , the entire Portuguese Air Force consisted of a Ford Tri-motor (resembling an old US mail carrier), two Hurricane fighters, a Spitfire, and a Fiesler Storch observation plane. Adding the P-47s would increase their air defense capacity tenfold.

When the pilots were trained and checked out for the P-47, the next hurdle was communicating tactical doctrines used by the US Air Force while the trainees were in the air. It was a real language problem, and to help overcome it, I decided to live with a middle-class family whose only language was Portuguese. It was a delightful but arduous experience. There was a mom, a dad, two young daughters, a toddler son, and a sweet, gray-haired grandmother. True to my wishes, none of them spoke a word of English. I ate meals with them and helped wash the dishes. I tried to speak with their children. They welcomed me in all of their conversations. At the same time I took private Portuguese lessons from a man who also taught English for the tourist business in the Algarve. After six weeks of enjoyable, often frustrating, total immersion language school, I acquired a basic knowledge of Portuguese—enough I hoped to communicate with the pilots in the air.

• • •

As commanding officer of their American advisor group, I often had lunch with the Portuguese base commander and their pilots. Those meals were always a sumptuous affair, and as custom dictated, they all drank a lot of wine. Everything was fine except for the wine part, so one day I broached the subject with the base commander. I told him as their advisor we couldn't allow pilots to drink wine before flying because it was obviously very dangerous. He agreed and promised to do something about it. Apparently my request came too late, because two days later one of their pilots was killed when he crashed his plane. It was obvious that his reactions had been dulled from all the wine he drank before taking off. I immediately went to the base commander.

"All planes are grounded," I ordered, "until you discontinue serving alcohol at lunch." He stopped it immediately.

Lunch with the Portuguese team, 1952

• • •

Although I knew Casey and the children were safe and well cared for by loving people in Kansas City, I missed her terribly. It had been five months since I left, and I wanted her to be with me. Since I was on a leave of absence without salary from American Thread, my Air Force pay didn't cover extras. Nevertheless, I managed to borrow $500 to pay for her airfare and other essentials, so she left our kids in the care of their grandparents and flew over to join me.

We lived in the same hotel with the rest of my team and the Portuguese flyers, and it worked out fine. Casey taught the Portuguese how to make pancakes, and they taught her how to make a few of their dishes, although she didn't take much to their food, particularly the seafood. We had a great time travelling around Portugal on weekends and holidays on our little Lambretta, a double-seated motor scooter. When it came to other days off, the Portuguese weren't all that excited about the war in Korea and didn't sense the urgency of establishing an air force. The result was a three-day weekend twice a month, so with all that time off we actually had a fine second honeymoon.

BACK TO THE THREAD COMPANY

In October 1952 the US role of establishing a Portuguese Air Force was over. Given the choice between air or sea transport, our unit elected to return to the States by ship—my fourth Atlantic crossing. Upon arrival, we were assigned to the Fort Dix Air Base in New Jersey.

Except for having our children with us again, Fort Dix was not a very happy time for Casey. Housing was in great demand, so all we could find was a two-room, cinderblock house in the middle of a field, in the middle of nowhere. Fortunately, we only had to stay there for the six weeks it took me to separate from active duty. When I was discharged yet again, we packed our things in a trailer and drove back to Connecticut and my job at the American Thread Company, picking up where we left off. We bought a house in Windham Center, the same town as before. It felt as small as a dollhouse, but since it was built in 1776, it had a lot of colonial charm.

My family enjoyed our life there, but I quickly became disenchanted with the American Thread Company. Maybe my experience with the National Guard and our time in Portugal gave me a different perspective, but I could see the company wasn't going anywhere. In fact, my accounting background and common marketing sense showed me the company was going downhill instead. Nevertheless, I stayed with them so I would have a more convincing résumé.

In 1957—two years after our son, Thomas, was born and one year after our third daughter, Patricia came into the world—I managed a transfer to American Thread's New York facility as their production manager. It seemed like a good move for the company and for me at the time. We moved to Ridgewood, New Jersey, just outside of New York City. The kids went to a school close to our sizable, three-story home with a basement.

KEEPING THE SPENCERS SAFE

Since I spent time in the National Guard during the Korean conflict, I was able to view the threat of nuclear war perhaps a bit closer than the average US citizen. Since I worked and lived very near to New York City, I was keenly aware that it would be an epicenter of a nuclear warhead. The common belief in the late fifties was a nuclear strike wouldn't extend too far beyond the immediate vicinity of ground zero. But, *not too far* was a misnomer. Our house in New Jersey was about twenty miles from Manhattan, so in my estimation we were directly in the line of fire. If I only had myself to worry about, I wouldn't have paid it much attention. Now, however, I had a wife and four children, so I determined to do all I could to keep them safe. That's when I, along with countless other Americans, decided to build a bomb shelter.

Our house had a large, deep basement with thick cement walls and a sturdy ceiling, which made it a good place for a bunker. Another benefit was the cool storage capacity, so we could have access to semi refrigerated food within arm's reach. Based on current information, the effects of a nuclear blast would last around four days.

Using four-by-four studs and plywood, I built a mold and filled it in with concrete, resulting in a wall about a foot wide all around the sides and the top. Then I installed a heavy steel door and ran a filtered ventilation pipe up through the roof to the outside. When I was done, there was just enough room for the six of us to sit and wait. I eventually planned to install bunks along the walls for all of us. I also stored canned or packaged food inside, as well as several gallons of water. As for the toilet, well, we didn't have one. We'd have to use a bucket or something, and designate one of the kids to dump it outside the bunker on a regular basis. Just who would clean up the area after the all-clear was given was yet to be determined. Now it was time to practice taking shelter.

One Saturday evening after dinner, and without letting my family know, I called out, "Hit the bomb shelter!" Everyone knew what that meant, so we scrambled toward the basement, grabbing whatever books or snacks we could along the way. Minutes later, we stood all safe and sound inside the dimly lit cubicle, which was about the size of a triple-walk-in closet. We tried the drill a few more times, until I thought we were prepared for whatever Mr. Khrushchev might do.

One night we had a cocktail party in our house, and one of the neighbors who came had two children around the same age as one of our kids. The mother said, "I heard you have a bomb shelter down in your basement. My daughter, Susie, told me all about it."

"Yes," I said, "we do have one. Would you like to see it?"

We went downstairs, and I turned on the light so she could look around. She seemed impressed.

"Well," she said, "what would you do if a missile was on the way, and our son, Peter, was at your house with your son, Tom? What if he was scared and wanted to get in with the rest of you?"

I answered with the straightest face I could muster. "Well, I'd probably have to shoot him."

To this day I am still on her shit list.

• • •

In addition to the threat of nuclear war, I was very concerned about a fire in our house. Our sixteen-year old, three-story home was made of wood, and Tom's room was on the top floor. If we had a fire of any magnitude, Tom wouldn't be able to get out because his only escape route was a wooden staircase down to the second floor. To remedy that threat, I developed a handy, knotted rope he could throw from his rather large window and use to shinny down to safety.

I bought forty feet of two-inch rope and tied a knot every three feet or so to give him something to grab on to. Tom was not only not frightened at the prospect, he actually saw is as some kind of an adventure. He could hardly wait for the fire drill. As for the rest of the family, they thought it was hilarious. We held our first drill, and the rest of the Spencer family gathered on the lawn to watch Tom make his way down the rope. He did it with ease and loved the experience.

From that time forward, I occasionally called a fire drill to be sure all systems were in place. Well, the word got out through the neighborhood that Spencer had his son climb from the third-story window in a mock fire situation, and people began to gather to see the spectacle.

"Hey everybody, Spencer's having another fire drill!" they'd yell. Several of them showed up with lawn chairs and drinks. A few of them were aghast. "Mike, you shouldn't make that little kid of yours do that, you know."

"Yeah," I replied, "but someday that just might save his life."

But they still stayed to enjoy the show. My fire drill became a regular event for our Ridgewood community.

• • •

Five years after rejoining American Thread, I realized yet again the company wouldn't last very long, no matter what division I worked in. After investing nine good years in that company, I knew it was time to find another opportunity. This time though, I wouldn't rush into a job, but instead carefully assess the qualities of the position before making a decision—the way I did before asking Casey to dance.

≡ 3 ≡

MARBON CHEMICALS, AUSTRALIA

I signed up with a New York City consultant who taught me how to write a résumé and be effective in an oral interview. I spent an enormous amount of money on him—over $800 in 1963 money—but it was worthwhile. After a year with Casey's help in typing, and over one hundred applications, I received eight responses from potential employers. The one that really caught my attention was a company named Marbon Inc., a large chemical conglomerate based in Parkersburg, West Virginia. After further investigation, I verified Marbon was an aggressive, growth-oriented company—my most important criteria. I targeted the production manager position in their chemical processing division with eleven hundred employees. It called for a degree in chemical engineering or a qualified chemist with several years of experience in the industry. Although I lacked some of the qualifications, they apparently liked what I had to offer.

Over the course of several interviews (and thanks to my consultant), I avoided the topic of my degree and instead focused on what I had to offer in their production, planning, and facility operations areas. Apparently I convinced them because they hired me to work under a gentleman named Len Harvey, a good man whom I worked with for several years in various positions in the company.

I started out as a planning manager and, within a year, became a production manager. Two years later, I was promoted to plant manager, overseeing those eleven hundred employees who worked three shifts seven days per week. As my stature in the company increased, so did my skills as a manager, planner, and negotiator. The latter would be put to the test every time our employees tried to unionize—something Marbon did not want to happen.

THE UNIONS

Relatively few employees really wanted to unionize. Those who did were the ones I believed would be unhappy with their job regardless of the pay or working conditions. However, every two or three years, a groundswell of complaints grew to the point where they decided to put it to a vote: whether to unionize or not. Every time that happened, I met with their leaders individually or spoke with them in groups in what amounted to a town-hall meeting. Most of the time, our conversations were civil, but sometimes we got into some heavy arguments.

Their complaint was always about pay. That was interesting because Marbon, as one of several chemical companies along the Ohio River (a.k.a. Chemical River), paid the same wage as the others or more. Most of our employees knew they could talk with me if they felt they weren't getting fair pay. In response I always tried to meet their needs, but there were always a few who wanted more.

As the date of the vote drew near, I continued to meet with the employees to discuss the logic of what they were about to do. I also spoke with the aspiring union boss.

"What would a union really do for your fellow employees?" I asked. "They're going to pay $500 or so every month just to be a member of your union, and what will they get for that money?"

I told him to think it over because if he became the union boss, he would have a big responsibility for the workers way beyond his own personal desire. I asked the employee groups the same thing:

"How much would you have to pay in monthly union dues? Would it make a difference in your take home pay at the end of the year?"

Discussions often went long into the evening, and they usually took the same route. By that time they thought it through, there was never a majority in favor of unionizing. In every case, it wasn't as if the company tried to take advantage of our employees. We couldn't, because labor relations were very transparent in the Ohio Valley, and we all had to take good care of our people, union or not.

That was part of my job as plant manager. If the periodic union discussions were tedious for me at the time, they would pay off in a big way later on.

• • •

My experience in Europe during the war and later in Portugal must have inspired me to see more of the world than Parkersburg, West Virginia. Consequently, when the rumor spread that Marbon planned to build an operation in Australia, I told those higher up in the company hierarchy that I would be the ideal person to organize and manage the project. At first, they were reticent, but eventually they agreed. In 1967 Casey, Tom, Chris, Patty, and I packed our things and moved to Australia. My daughter, Gina, who was in college at the time, joined us later on. On the way over we stopped at Fiji for a few days and then Hawaii. We rented a house in Australia outside of Melbourne, and a year later bought a home in North Baldwyn, a high-quality, family-oriented neighborhood with leafy streets outside of the city where we lived until 1971.

Prior to my transfer to Australia, Marbon had shipped high-impact plastic products to Australia for further processing for various applications through an agent called M.E. Holmes. As business grew, corporate decided a lot more money could be made by establishing a factory there instead of sending our products halfway around the world. Additionally, Australia lacked sufficient technical expertise to grow both products and the market, and we were in a better position to establish our own company. Marbon Chemicals, USA, went on to establish a joint venture with an Australian company with plans to build a factory.

In the eyes of the Australians living in Dandenong, where the factory would be built, a large American petrochemical plant meant job security for them. *(Dandenong was a country town with more sheep than people.)* On the political side, our joint venture was a win-win for both the Aussies and the Americans. The plant was done ahead of schedule, and when it opened, it went gangbusters.

• • •

Acrylic Styrene was a low-impact plastic, which, if dropped, tended to shatter. To remedy the situation, Marbon scientists developed a way to integrate a rubber compound into the mix to make it bounce instead of break. The result was ABS, and once it hit the market, it really took off.

Our biggest customer was Western Union, the folks who made all those telephones back in the day. When more and more of the phones found their way into homes and the workplace, another benefit of ABS was discovered almost by accident. Our marketing people heard that women in particular liked the phone, but not because it didn't break if it got dropped on a tile floor. They liked it because they could easily wipe their lipstick off the mouthpiece. The old brittle plastic absorbed the lipstick, but ABS was slick. One swipe of a hanky cleared up all the red stuff.

The success of ABS and other products brought growth and prosperity to Marbon Australia. And like most organizations experiencing growth, it came with the potential of labor unrest—nothing serious, but enough to disrupt an otherwise fine-tuned enterprise. Therefore, much of my job as managing director was to keep employer-employee relations in good health. I poured all my energy into that aspect of the job, and over time, the result was very low turnover—about 3 percent—because no one wanted to leave. According to many employees, their reasons for staying were due to "little things that make a big difference." I suppose one reason was my philosophy of people management as described in a few publications during my tenure. One Australian business magazine put it like this:

> Egalitarian is perhaps the best word to describe Mr. Michael Spencer. His deep interest in people, his conviction that they can attain higher goals, and his personal identification with every employee, draws upon his strong egalitarian principles. But at the same time, he never loses sight of his responsibility to shareholders.

The article went on to explain how.

> But the man who is going to make the multimillion dollar investment work is perhaps more interesting. His philosophies are homespun. Some will no doubt say too homespun. One should realize of course that a giant international company such as Marbon does not brief an executive who is living in a cotton wool world to set up a production plant in Australia. It briefs a man with managerial and technical knowhow, organizational ability, experience, flair, and dynamism. That Mike Spencer was briefed to set up a grass roots plant in Australia is Marbon's tangible acknowledgment that he

possesses these qualities. And there are more, if these
are not enough. He is learning Japanese because he
foresees the growing contact with them. "They know
English," he said, "I should know Japanese."

Another article quoted me on what I believed was key for
employee motivation.

"It's easy to put even the office boy in a box at the bottom
of an organizational chart, but anyone in this position
is likely to get a giant-sized inferiority complex seeing
all those boxed above him. Setting out our operations
in the form of a wheel seems to make everyone more
conscious of the fact that they are part of a team and
not boxes on the bottom of the list, supporting a great
mass of overheads."

I practiced my egalitarian attitude in tangible ways, too. Even
though I was the managing director of the company, I didn't have
my own company parking space. That's how much I wanted our
organizational chart to be a level playing field. If I wanted the best
spot, I had to get to work before everyone else. I played up things like
that since we were all in the business together. I didn't want them to
think there were some at the top shouting orders at them. I could do
that, but I knew that wouldn't work. My chosen leadership approach
was best described as egalitarian, and after promoting it a while, it
caught on. People respected it and in turn applied it to their own
situations.

Happy people do more work than unhappy people, and unhappy
people always look for a way out of doing their jobs. At Marbon
Australia, I tried to create an atmosphere where people knew they
were highly valued. I illustrated that with my circular organization

chart, where the relationships showed people as people, not just a name in a hierarchy. Nor did we keep secrets from our people. If we were going to make some kind of important change, we talked to the employees first. This practice helped when we were faced with a need, such as a tight deadline. If we had to double up to get things out the door in time, we asked the staff to work overtime, and they almost always agreed.

⚌ 4 ⚌

IT BEGAN IN THE COCKPIT

During my time with Marbon, I grew professionally and personally. It is at this juncture that I depart from my career and focus on another side of my life—my spiritual self. Although Casey was raised as a Catholic and I was a Protestant, neither she nor her family made an issue of my non-Catholic background. She did make sure our children went to church on Sundays, which was fine with me. I occasionally went along with them, but I never felt sitting in a church building did much for my spiritual life. That began to change after I started to talk with the local Catholic priest in Dandenong, Australia.

My spiritual transformation happened when I was at church with my wife and kids. The Catholic Church had recently decided to omit Latin from their services and use English instead. The priest opened the service by explaining the meaning of the change and how the English language would be involved in their faith. When he began to recite from his book, I found myself saying the same words as he was without looking at the text. My daughter, Regina, looked at me with a surprised expression and asked, "Dad, how do you know that? How come you can say what he's saying?" I told her I learned it in a Protestant church, and that the priest actually spoke from what we called the Book of Common Prayer. The switch from Latin to English was quite a change for long-time Catholics, but to me it made perfect sense. From that Sunday on, I talked with the priest as often as I could, and not long after that, I decided to join the church.

Actually, my deeper journey of faith started long before I became a Catholic. It happened that day in the cockpit of my P-47 when I was hit by that flak train and thought I was going down. When the engine failed, and I went through the emergency checklist with no results, I asked him to help me. When he—or the impression of some superior being—said, "Check the fuel transfer pump," I knew something big had taken place. I realized that was the first *impulse* —I suppose I could call it that—I had about any religion. Something had changed. It wasn't as if I suddenly wanted to join a new church, but I definitely experienced a new feeling about religion, and I had to check it out. However pure my intentions were, though, my spiritual journey was soon trumped by everyday life. After the war I got married, finished college, had kids, and pursued my career. My religious life again took a back seat.

Years later I read about religion and philosophy but never talked with anyone about it. I read the Koran, which I found interesting, and discovered that much of what it said was also in the Bible. I read the Bible when I was a boy, and read the New Testament from start to finish. Later, I spent about three and a half years reading the entire Bible again, which helped a lot. Then I read more philosophy, which seemed very similar in many ways to the Bible. As I entered my adult years, I relied on philosophy and its teaching about wisdom and understanding of relationships among people, the world, and what direction to take in life. I liked the Stoic philosopher Epictetus, who taught that philosophy was a way of life, not just a theoretical discipline. To him, all external events are beyond our control, so we should accept whatever happens calmly and dispassionately. He also taught that people are still responsible for their actions and should exercise control through self-discipline. In some ways the Bible has similar teachings.

During the period between the epiphany in the cockpit and when I became a Catholic, I tried to take God away from the supernatural. That didn't mean I trivialized Him, because I believed God was, and is, available on a practical, daily basis. I don't look to Him as some magician who lives way beyond, but as One with whom I can have a unique relationship. Having said that, it's still difficult to completely describe my faith at this point. I've been a Catholic for some time now, but if someone would ask me to explain my beliefs or what the meaning of a certain passage of Scripture is, I can only say my Christianity is more practical than that. That means I rely on it, and God, all the time.

THE NETHERLANDS

Holland, 1971

Several years after I took over at Marbon Australia, a major explosion occurred in our Marbon Netherlands plant. It was the kind of event that required a specialist in developing chemical plants to get the operation up and going again, so they asked me to transfer there to get things back on track. By that time, Marbon Australia was doing very well, and I felt the challenge was an opportunity to grow within the company. I accepted the offer, and soon my family and I found ourselves on a different continent.

Marbon Australia was a great experience, but Marbon Netherlands was just the opposite. A year after I arrived, it was apparent I did not get the support I needed nor the independence required to operate as general manager and vice president of operations. It was a strange situation: rebuilding plant operations after a devastating fire was no small job, yet neither the president of Marbon Europe nor Howard Irvin, president of the international division of Borg Warner Chemicals (our group owner), paid any attention. My hands were tied, and I decided to resign.

American Club Ball, Holland, 1972

After that, my friend and colleague George Fincham suggested that he and I start a company to help American companies get established in Australia. At that point, I knew a good deal about

Australian and American business practices and Australian land-purchase procedures, and George knew a lot about a lot of things in the area. We decided on a course of action, and in early 1974, Casey and I left Holland to return to Australia. As was our habit, we took advantage of the transition to travel and explore, so we visited Iran, Afghanistan, and India along the way.

BACK IN AUSTRALIA

Melbourne, Australia, 1978

A few months after George and I opened shop, we realized that the whole world was not moving to Australia, at least not as quickly as we had hoped, so we decided to dissolve our company, Site Services, LLC, and go our separate ways. My core competencies at the time were planning, consulting, and business operations, so I opened my own consulting business. It was fairly successful but not all that exciting, so I treated it as a temporary income-generator instead of a full-time career while I considered my future. Then I received a call from George McNally, president of Borg Warner Chemicals. George asked me if I'd be interested in returning to the company to start an operation in Asia for them. He said I'd be based in Hong Kong.

It didn't take long for me to say I'd be interested. In fact, I was thrilled. Just because things didn't go well in Holland didn't mean this would happen in Asia. It would be a different team running the operation in Asia and the Pacific Rim. Casey was as excited as I, so we closed everything down, sold the house (Casey sold the cars), and left Australia.

HONG KONG

We arrived in Hong Kong in early 1980, a period when many companies in the United States had become serious about doing business in Asia. As such, Hong Kong was even more congested and the demand for good housing was sky high, so it was almost impossible to find a good place to live. We had no other option than to check in to the Hilton Hotel on Hong Kong Island. We ate out every night at the best restaurants and enjoyed all the extra free time we had together. Casey explored the city and found out where to shop while I sourced an office location and organized the company. The Hilton was a very nice place, but with only two rooms it became a little cramped.

When we first arrived in Hong Kong, our real estate agent told us about a new development in Kowloon that would be complete in about five months. If we put our names on a waiting list, we would get a wonderful apartment in few months. Thirteen months later we checked out of the Hilton and moved in. The wait was worth it.

The apartment was twenty-nine hundred square feet of luxurious living space. We had marble and wood floors, modern appliances, spacious bathrooms and kitchen, and a fabulous view of the Hong Kong harbor from the balcony, where we enjoyed drinks as the sun set in the west.

Casey, Regina and me, Hong Kong, 1981

Shortly after we moved in, Casey spoke with a friend who was leaving the city. She said their Philippine housekeeper, called an *Amah*," needed a new place to work. Her friend thought we would be a good match for her, so, Hilda (not much of a Philippine name, but she liked it) joined us shortly after her former employers left. *Filipinas* preferred to work for people like us since we had separate rooms with a shower for them. Most others had to sleep on the floor of their English or American clients.

Hilda was the best Amah anyone could hope for. She was an accomplished chef who prepared American, Philippine, and Chinese food, and she did them all very well. She also enjoyed keeping everything in the house shipshape: my clothes were always pressed; my shoes were shined; she did laundry every day. Hilda's efficiency gave Casey time to get out of the house to enjoy the city. In fact, Casey liked to say she retired long before I did.

We were in Hong Kong eight full, enjoyable years. I traveled widely throughout Asia, visiting every country as far west as Pakistan. I grew to know Asia well and frequently took Casey with me. I count those years as among the best in my career.

• • •

The years between the end of World War II and when I finished my contract with Borg Warner absolutely flew by. I enjoyed my role as plant manager, consultant, business development specialist, and trainer in various parts of the world. When I wasn't working or spending time with Casey and our kids, I studied foreign languages, such as Japanese and Russian. I took Dale Carnegie courses, and when I graduated they asked me to become one of their instructors. Casey and I watched our four children thrive in an international environment that enriched their life experiences. I'm proud to say they all turned out very well indeed. I enjoyed success with my family, my jobs, and our relationships in the United States and abroad. Overall, I have been extremely blessed and very thankful for my life. At that point I was determined to not let it come to an end. After all, a rich, prosperous life is about staying interested, learning, experiencing, and growing.

Hong Kong, 1983

Hong Kong New Years, 1983

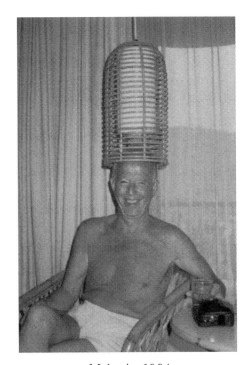

Malaysia, 1984

Bali, 1985

Egypt, 1985

Christmas, 1986

Making fudge with grandchildren, Ginny and Spencer, 1989

With Patty, 1995

Our 50th Wedding Anniversary, 1996

With granddaughter, Addie, 2000

TRANSITIONS

I was about to retire in 1987 when the officers of Borg Warner Chemicals decided to allow a management buyout. The action destroyed a lot of my plans when they asked me to help some of the other Borg Warner divisions become familiar with the Chinese business culture so they could determine the best opportunities. For the next two years I traveled extensively throughout the world visiting various BW divisions, consulting with them as to the best approach to the new market.

When that phase of my work was done, Casey and I prepared to leave Hong Kong. Now we had to find a good place to retire, but we didn't know where since we'd seen so many beautiful places in the world. We were impressed with a little beach town we once visited in Florida, a place named Ponte Vedra. My brother, and sister-in-law, Bob and Marguerite Spencer, had settled there years before, so we thought we'd pay them a visit to test the water, so to speak. We flew to Ponte Vedra in 1987, and after staying a week we were even more impressed. Casey and I decided to retire there. We flew back to Hong Kong and arranged for our pending move.

The shipping agent told us to expect that it would take five weeks for our things to arrive in Florida, but once the ship left Australia, we heard it would take much longer than that, so of course, we did a little traveling on our way. After we arrived in Florida, we house hunted for a while and finally decided on a nice house in a suburb named Cyprus Creek. For the next eighteen years, Casey, I, and our visiting children shared many wonderful memories. It was a fabulous place to live, and everything about Ponte Vedra was better than we expected.

• • •

I have a plaque beneath the portrait of my wife on my office wall that reads, "It doesn't matter where you go in life: it's who you have by your side." When I traveled throughout the world with my job, I sometimes took my wife along, but usually I couldn't, and I'd be gone for a two or three weeks at a time. When I returned home Casey always welcomed me with wide, open arms. She made me feel like a twenty-two year-old all over again. There was never any of that, "Did you behave yourself?" It was always a happy time when we celebrated our reunion, and we usually went out to dinner or something fun to celebrate.

That kind of relationship—that feeling—is what I'd call regenerative. She was deeply in love with me, and I was deeply in love with her. It was a perfect marriage in every way by my standards. She taught me a lot about compassion and understanding of other people. She was also very wise about our children and how to raise them well. Casey frequently suggested things I could do as a father for our four kids: things I should do a little differently. I took her advice because I respected her insights.

Early in 2000, Casey began to suffer a considerable loss of memory. In the early stages, I could see something was affecting her memory, and in spite of the doctors and medications, it was obvious she wasn't going to make it. Then the illness came on faster and became very serious in a very short period of time. From then on our lives changed. She was still there even if she couldn't recall much of anything in her past. The ensuing years were trying, to say the least, but the whole family stayed close by while Casey and I lived out our last, loving years.

My life focused entirely on her well-being. My job was to do all I could to insure she was not in pain. We joked a lot and talked a lot. Of course, those eight years were nothing compared to the life we had together, but the quality of our love was stronger than ever. When she passed, it was probably as moderate as one could expect death to be. Now I don't spend a lot of time missing her, because we had so many years of wonderful memories—sixty-three to be exact. I can only be grateful I had them at all.

What did I learn from such loss? Love is a very important part of life, well-being, longevity, and meaning. Some would say love is everything, and I'm inclined to agree. How do I describe love? It's a feeling that cannot be described with my inadequate vocabulary. It's a feeling that grows and changes. If nurtured well, it gets better and better with time. *Love* is also a verb, meaning it is more action than feeling, a thing done even when we don't feel like doing it. As Casey neared her end, she said something very dear in a brief moment of clarity:

"Mike, we had a marvelous love affair, didn't we?"

"Yes," I said, "we sure did. And I wouldn't change a thing."

In January 2008, Casey and I danced for the last time.

With Casey at Tom and Mandy's Wedding, 1999

Part V

PLANS FOR MY FUTURE

(or How to Live a Satisfying Old Age)

══ 1 ══

BASIC INGREDIENTS

Way back when I was sixty-five, I felt I had control of my life. Everything was good. I ate and slept well and felt good. Today at the age of ninety-six, I'm happy to say not all that much has changed. The reason might be that somewhere along the line, I began to ask myself, "Why not think and feel the same way I did at sixty-five? Just because the calendar says I've racked up this many years, doesn't mean I have to feel that old."

Well, I don't. And I'm convinced that everyone approaching an advanced age can think and feel younger in the same way. To accomplish such a mindset requires attention to a basic set of tools. They are:

1. attitude,
2. physical exercise,
3. mental exercise,
4. diet,
5. medical attention,
6. relationships, and
7. genes.

The last one—genes—is the only tool over which we have little control. While just about everyone is familiar with these tools, the crux of implementing positive changes lies in the execution: one must actually *do* them. If you're blessed with good genes, great! If not, I believe if you stick to the remaining six main ingredients for good health, you can live for an indefinite period of time. That's what I believe, and that's what I intend to do. Having said that, I realize there are exceptions. There are many out there with no control over sickness, disease, accidents, or problems inherited at birth. All I can say is to exercise as many of the criteria I listed and do all you can to achieve a long, quality life.

Here's where it gets hard. Every one of these ingredients requires discipline a certain 'glue' for them to apply. For as long as I can remember, an inner voice told me, "I should be doing this or that." These subliminal prompts were always directed toward better health, and I suppose I placed them in my life's repertoire at a very young age. Contrary to the belief that discipline is a series of "thou shalt nots," my disciplines were actually "thou-shalts." I knew inside I should do whatever was necessary to maintain strength and health in order to lead a long life.

Playing tennis with daughters and grandchildren, 2014

IT'S MOSTLY HOW YOU THINK

I believe the way one thinks about old age in their early life will impact how they feel when they actually get there. "Old" is not a bad word in and of itself. It becomes bad when people—young people in particular—relate negatively with individuals who have lived for so many years. Because our society looks to youth as basically good and to old age as basically not so good, everyone, including seniors, tends to believe that untruth. The numbers on my wall calendar might say I'm old, but those are just numbers on a sheet of paper. The way I see it, if I feel old in parts of my body, I don't go out the door in the morning thinking, "Oh, I've got a limp so I've got to avoid doing this or that today." That kind of thinking results in gearing back on my activities until I don't do much at all. Such a defeatist attitude must be avoided at all costs. Instead, I ignore the pain, walk out my door, and keep moving.

For those who grew up fearing old age, I have this to say: "Don't accept old age as a measure of your life". Your body can keep going and your mind can keep going if you want them to. You have to tell yourself, "Old age is not old age by any other measure than the calendar." Okay, so the pages of the calendar drop, and you're another year older. The next thing you might think is, "Since I'm older, I probably can't do certain things any longer." Now you have an attitude problem. Who said you can't? How do they know? Instead, tell yourself, "I can do everything I want to do."

From my perspective, I know things are different now than they were when I was younger, but I don't have to accept the prescribed limitations of age just because society says so. Tell yourself you're going to keep living. Repeat it to yourself over and over again. Don't prepare yourself to die; prepare yourself to live. Why limit yourself when there is something you can do about it?

That goes for your mental capacity too. Scientists have concluded that the brain does not begin to atrophy at age twenty-eight, as they formerly believed. In fact, your brain keeps regenerating as time goes on. All that stuff you tucked in your gray matter throughout your life doesn't just go away: it's still there. If you fail to remember something, you probably haven't needed the information for quite a while anyway. I speak from personal experience because I was amazed with the details I remembered while writing this book. The brain is like a muscle: when you exercise it, good things happen.

Your attitude affects your sex life as well. No one should believe that because the calendar says a man or woman is of a certain age that sex goes out the window. That's simply not true, even at age ninety-six. We all have wonderfully made bodies and if we take good care of them, sex is possible at any age. Most people who say it's impossible don't know what they're talking about. Even if they assert it might be possible but not much fun, they're still full of baloney! Where did they get their information? If you ask them if they have firsthand information, they'll probably say, "Well, no, but my grandfather so-and-so said there's no sex after eighty." Just look at recent statistics about life in many retirement homes. The accounts read like a toned-down version of *Fifty Shades of Grey*. If these naysayers want to put themselves in the old-age category and believe sex is no longer possible, let them do it. They've already talked themselves out of it.

Tell yourself you have a body and a mind and a life, and you intend to enjoy it. Sure, some limitations happen, but people can still feel the joy of living. If not, what's the alternative?

IT'S NOT JUST THE WRAPPER

A lot of people are hung up on their physical appearance. The image they saw in the mirror when they were young determined the way they felt about life, and when they grew older they tended to develop self-image problems. Youthful appearance always gives way to sags and bags, and if physical appearance is all one lives for, it can be very depressing. Depression leads to giving up, which leads to further deterioration. That is a terrible downward spin that is difficult to overcome. The only way around this downward spiral is to realize everyone is in the same boat and that aging is a natural process.

Ziplining in Costa Rica, 2014

With proper attitude and physical management, youthful good looks can transcend to an inward vitality that comes through as true beauty. Have you ever encountered an older person who is happy, sold out on life, who enjoys the moment? We are left with a good feeling about who they are and how they affected us more than what they looked like. What we saw was their spirit, their attitude. They weren't born with such vitality: they nourished it throughout their life. That's good news for you and me because through discipline and a good attitude, we can all achieve the same kind of joy.

Is your physical self the only thing keeping you motivated? If so, you're on the road to depression. If, on the other hand you engage everyday life as a series of opportunities and have a grateful, optimistic outlook, you will lay a foundation for a life of quality and meaning that can take you well into your eighties, nineties, and beyond. I pity those who reach "old age" and sit around just waiting for death. That's a ridiculous way to live! Start right now. Don't be so concerned about the nit-picking physical details that can blunt your joy. Depression shortens life, but you can live longer if you consider each day as a cherished gift.

2

ON SURVIVAL

I am just about the only survivor among my peers. I suppose I could be distressed by that fact, but I look at it as something to be grateful for. It doesn't mean I think I'm the next one to die, it means I'm still alive and strong. Being a survivor is another form of the discipline I addressed earlier.

Besides my war experiences, I have survived some very difficult situations at other times, such as when I lost my daughter, Chris, in an automobile accident in January, 1977. While it was unbelievably devastating as a father to lose a child, the event didn't bring my life to an end. I suppose it was another situation when my strong faith in life eventually overcame my grief. Of course, there are countless people who survive in the same way, but the pivotal factor is how they get on with life after a disaster. Being a survivor can create strength if one is inclined to accept it as a discipline. In my case, accepting it as such enabled me to live on.

A WORD ABOUT GOALS

I mentioned earlier that I have plans for my life. And because I have plans, I have faith that I'll be around to see my plans come to fruition.

I believe they will materialize, and because I believe this, I build certain goals into my daily life that will guide me in that direction. I do things that reflect that future reality, and as a result I organize my life accordingly. Does that make sense? A goal is an added ingredient to life, and it works wonders to make my time on more than just an existence. Goals mean *purpose*, which is something to cherish.

For example, one goal I established was to write my autobiography and finish it before Christmas 2016, which I did. Another goal is to discover how my brain works, which I've always been curious about. To achieve that goal, at least in part, I'm working through a book titled *The Secrets of Mental Health*. I'm also fascinated by the Chinese language, so I regularly dig into the topic. Then there's the literary side of me. I've always wanted to write in a serious way, so another goal of mine is to learn how to write creative nonfiction. To that end I'm listening to an audio book entitled *Writing Creative Nonfiction* and reading a print book entitled *Building a Better Vocabulary*.

If all this seems strange, consider Grandma Moses who started painting in earnest at the relatively young age of seventy-eight. She did pretty well far into her late eighties. Since I plan to live to at least until 102, I've got some time to do what I plan, right? Exactly what I'll contribute to society with all that remains to be seen, but I'll enjoy the journey.

Goals also help ward off depression, a disease affecting countless people of all ages in this country. When I begin to feel unhappy (the first stage of depression), I'll sit at my piano and play a melody. I'm not all that good on the keys, but I can play Brahms's "Cradle Song" very well. I'll play it over and over again until I'm back on track.

When I sense the specter of unhappiness, I always take action to keep it away. I never give in to it, and because I don't, it never becomes a problem. The key is to see it for what it is and prevent it from ruining even one moment of my life. When things don't go right, as they sometimes don't, I ask myself, "Why should it bother me? I've lived through many calendar years, and most anything that comes my way has already happened at least once. I survived it, so why let it get to me now?"

IT REALLY IS WHAT YOU EAT

I have an acquaintance at my gym who occasionally asks, "Mike, you seem to be doing everything at your old age. How can you do it?" I interrupt him mid-sentence and say, "Hold on, Charlie, I'm not old. I'm just Mike Spencer. According to the calendar I've spent ninety-six years on this planet, but beyond that I have no concept of age because I refuse to be old by your standards."

"Well, yeah," he responds, "but it's still hard being old."

When I hear things like that, I smile and say something like this: "Look, if you can stand on your own two feet (he has a hard time walking), you can make yourself walk straight instead of shuffling along. It might hurt a bit, but you can do it because your body can do more than you realize. Start thinking like you're sixty-five instead of ninety-five. Make that your mindset and just do it."

When he doesn't respond, I give him more advice.

"Be careful what you eat. Don't give up on fruits, nuts, and vegetables. Drink lots of water. Take your medications, but try to work yourself off of them eventually. See your doctor regularly. Eat tomatoes—lots of them. I eat tomatoes now even though I hated them all my life because I know they're good for me."

═ 3 ═

WHEN THE PHYSICAL SELF WON'T COOPERATE

I keep a parallel beam in the middle of my front room. It's about ten feet long and stands about one foot off the carpet. Every time I walk from my office to the kitchen, I step on the beam and practice walking, one foot in front of the other, to maintain my sense of equilibrium. Due to a bad knee, balance is a part of my somewhat incomplete self. I also practice balancing seven times a week at the gym on an inflated ball with a flat top. To me, balancing on that thing for only a few minutes is the equivalent of a one-mile walk. Uncomfortable? Sure. In fact, I don't like going to the gym at all, but the great way I feel afterwards makes it worthwhile

There is another way I look at physical health that may seem a little far-fetched. If I stay in the best possible shape until I reach 102, there's a good chance by then medical technology will have found a way to repair or replace most anything in our bodies: knees, elbows. ankles. organs. Eyes, you name it. Stem cell technology, robotics, and neuroscience are already breaking ground faster than the medical community can keep up. So as long as I keep my physical structure healthy, I'm convinced by the time I get to be 102, I won't have to worry. By then, healthcare providers may replace worn out body parts with new ones, or grow a new organ from scratch. If technology keeps developing that fast, why couldn't I live to be 150?

Some might say, "But nothing like that has ever happened before." Well, I can think of hundreds of things that weren't done before. Innovations will apply to medicine, too. Our bodies are God-given for sure, but I don't recall God ever telling me to give up keeping it in good shape. No, I'm looking forward to it because I'm not ready to leave this Earth just yet.

AFTER CALAMITY, MOVE ON!

The longer we live, the greater chance we have of losing someone dear. That's a given. When you lose a spouse in your advanced years, you often lose your purpose in life as well. I've seen that a lot, and while it's understandable, it should not mean the end of his joy. If you have established a healthy balance between your reliance on your spouse and on yourself during the marriage, when you're suddenly alone you should be able to live with a life of quality. Put another way, your general wellbeing will depend greatly on the quality of the relationship you had with your departed spouse.

I had a wonderful sixty-three-year relationship with Casey, and though it was difficult when she passed away, I am still able to continue my life. Today I can say I love life, have plans, goals, and a future. Knowing that Casey would be happy if I kept on with life (as I would for her if the situation was reversed), I have established a relationship with a lovely woman who has become my partner.

Lore speaks three languages and holds a PhD in psychology. She's an excellent conversationalist, and I find her level of education requires a bit of work for me to keep up with her, which is a good thing. We have a martini hour most every day around five, and we talk until dinner time. She's a fabulous cook, more like a chef, and she takes her time to prepare everything carefully. We also go on cruises together, and between the two of us we're fairly well traveled.

Although we enjoy each other's company very much, we decided never to get married or even live together. Being married at our age with our respective children, grandchildren, and nice homes, wouldn't add much to the relationship. Having said that, there is a chance that without marriage, our relationship might come to an end before I want it to. To hedge that eventuality, I told her if she finds another, younger man, he won't have all the abilities I have! *(She's only eighty-one.)*

Easter with Lore, 2012

My point is if people are unhappy being single in their older years, I believe it's important for them to find a mate. That won't work for everyone of course, particularly if they're content being single. Sometimes a new companion or spouse is more complicated than it should be. Regardless, the important thing is to keep exercising the criteria mentioned above and not give up.

· · ·

I don't want to sound greedy, but I have every intention of celebrating my 102nd birthday with my children and friends. That's only six years from the publication of this book, and I think that's fairly realistic. Why would I want to live that long? The answer is because I am a happy person. I enjoy life very much, and I'm not ready for it to end just yet.

Teaching Addie piano, 2010

Patricia's Wedding, 2013

With son-in-law Jon at Lake George, NY, 2015

Granddaughter Ginny's Wedding, 2015

With son Tom, receiving the
French Legion of Honour Medal, 2016

French Legion of Honour Certificate, 2016

Balancing on a bosu ball at age 95, 2016

Made in the USA
Middletown, DE
27 May 2018